A Place Called Surrender

Dan Roelofs

A Place Called Surrender
Second edition trade book
Copyright 2002, 2016 by Dan Roelofs

To order more books,
visit: www.aplacecalledsurrender.com
and: www.amazon.com

Second edition editorial:
Inspira Literary Solutions, Gig Harbor, WA
Second edition design:
Brianna Showalter, Ruston, WA
First edition editorial:
Sally Jenkins and Joanna Bursch
Cover design and photography by Mark Griffin

ISBN: 978-0-9979303-9-9

CONTENTS

FOREWORD TO THE FIRST EDITION

As a pastor of 30 years, I have ministered to many families who have faced the crisis that Dan and Tammy faced. I hate cancer. I don't even like the word. It sounds like sin and fits with everything else that is wrong in this world. Cancer is so indiscriminate. It affects little children, healthy adults, and the partners of lonely, elderly people. Cancer is not fair.

Dan and Tammy traveled with me doing conferences several times over the course of a couple years. We made memories together at the top of the Sears Tower in Chicago and on the streets of Manhattan while ministering in those cities. Every parent would want children like them. I wanted to stand them up in front of the church and say, "Here is what you get, Mom and Dad, if you do your job right." How could someone so morally good and as healthy as Dan Roelofs get cancer? Dan and Tammy were the epitome of what is right about life, about America, and about the Church.

Obviously, following Jesus does not ensure a problem-free life. Not even a life guaranteed to be free of tragedy or heartache. But as you will see in this book, it is often in the midst of heartache that God's voice is heard with greatest clarity.

7

Dan began recording his thoughts and feelings from the beginning of his journey. Then he started a website to inform those who were praying for him about his medical progress. My wife and I checked it every day. The medical issues were only a small part of the story. He also reported his spiritual journey. We were all blessed by his insights and maturity as he stared death in the face. Fortunately, Dan kept all that he wrote and compiled many of those insights in this little volume.

His Heavenly Father was with Dan Roelofs in every high and low period. That is what is right about this story, and what is right about life. God is our life, and Dan knew it.

This book is the record of a spiritual journey. You will cry, as I did, when you read it, but you will rejoice as well. Their story is a triumph of the Spirit in the midst of trials. Growth takes place in the valleys, and it is there that the Psalms come alive. Even though Dan walked through the valley of the shadow of death, he feared no evil, because the Good Shepherd was with him.

Dr. Neil T. Anderson
President Emeritus
Freedom In Christ Ministries

FOREWORD TO THE SECOND EDITION

Every so often a book comes along that does more than impact a reader for a moment; it actually creates a lasting movement in people's lives—like it did with our oldest daughter, Kari.

Kari was coming out of an abusive relationship, and had recently turned her life over to the Lord. While a lot of healing had happened, the concept of surrender was still foreign to her. My wife and I prayed as she battled to lay down the things she thought were best for her, and as she struggled to accept God's best.

In October of 2014, the message of this book grabbed hold of Kari's heart. For her, the story you'll read led to a deep and real understanding of God's ability to BE EVERYTHING, and the contentment and joy that comes when a heart KNOWS that Jesus really is enough, even in the toughest of times.

Since that day, Kari has not only grown more than we could imagine with the Lord, but has even started a ministry to help others do the same. She looks radiant, too. As it was for Dan and Tammy in this book, the "glow" found in surrender is contagious.

That's my view of what went on in Kari's life after

she read this book. Here are her thoughts, in her words, of what it meant to her...

When a dear friend gave me the book you are holding, I was in the middle of a crisis. I had been praying for clarity and direction, but was so stuck that I couldn't see any way out of the mess I was in. This book was a last resort.

I sat down in my cozy water-view apartment, planning to read only a few pages. However, I was quickly sucked into Dan's story. While I didn't have cancer, the raw and real emotions he and his family were experiencing hit so close to my heart. I HAD to see how this man found peace in his greatest season of chaos.

Over the next few hours I read the book three different times, through blurred tears and interspersed prayers of desperation. What I found in the following pages was completely life changing.

By the end of the book, I was convinced that Dan, and his family, truly believed that even if it meant death, he wanted to surrender to God's plan. They believed God was enough, God was good, and God was in control, no matter what the outcome was.

While you'll have to read the book to see how the story ends, I felt like someone had punched me in the gut. This man KNEW these things to be true about God.

Here I was, facing something much less intense than cancer, and I could not honestly say in my heart of hearts that I knew God was good. I was full of fear about the future and terrified that if I let God lead, I would hate the outcome. In that moment, I had a choice: ask God to help me surrender, or continue to try to do things on my own.

For months, I had been basically in depression, asking over and over how a God who loved me could allow me to go through so much pain. How could things go from amazing to impossible overnight? Had I disappointed God? Was I being punished?

I re-read the book and, I think for the first time, truly accepted God's plan as my own. As I surrendered, the Lord began to reach places in my heart that were broken, and address questions about His character. He showed me His incredible grace and love, humbled me, and eventually restored my identity. He answered every prayer and every cry of my heart in a deeper way than I ever could have imagined.

I pray that wherever you are at in your process—a season of fire, a season of fulfillment, or possibly a season where you don't know who God is yet—that you would allow yourself grace, and ASK the Lord to break through. He is faithful.

~Kari Trent

For what it meant to our daughter and so many others, we are so thankful for Dan Roelof's faithfulness, even in his darkest moments, in writing this book. We are also thankful for Tammy's faithfulness today in continuing to share her story of healing, redemption, and surrender. The impact of this family and their obedience goes far beyond what is even visible in the moment. We stand with them and pray that as you read this book, you, too, will be blessed and changed, and that you will experience the true joy and power that comes from surrender.

John Trent, Ph.D.
Best-Selling Author of *The Blessing*
President of StrongFamilies

ACKNOWLEDGMENTS

Today is Thanksgiving Day, 2002. It is also one year to the day since I was diagnosed with malignant melanoma. A year ago, I only hoped to experience this day with my family. My heart is gushing with thanks to God . . . for life, for His undying love, for the privilege of serving Him. If I were to fully express my gratitude on paper, this would be the longest section of the book. I'll refrain. However, there are some specific people I would like to thank.

Mom and Dad, it was your faith and the values you were passionate about that sustained me until the time when those same values could be my own. I could never thank you enough for the support that you have given me at every critical juncture in life. I can't imagine parents who love their kids more. (By the way, Mom, I am taking my vitamins.)

Mark and Rachel, I am proud to be your brother. I am even more proud to be able to tell people of the depth of love and passion you both have for

God. I am so thankful to God that you are not only my siblings, but also my friends.

Dave Park, thank you for believing in me and demonstrating that in a thousand ways. You have helped me to see myself in Christ. This book may never have come into existence apart from your prodding and encouragement. It has been and will be an incredible privilege to minister with you.

Woodland Fellowship, you have been the most gracious and supportive church family a pastor could ever have. Thank you for standing by us through thick and thin. Thank you for being the hands and feet of Jesus to us.

Mark Griffin and Sally Jenkins, I am so grateful that you chose to serve the Lord by coming alongside me in this project. You are both remarkably gifted, but humble. Thank you.

Ross Robinson, sometimes I think you know me better than I know myself. Your passion for God has fueled my own more times than I can count. I never knew a friendship could be so rich.

I will conclude by thanking you, Tammy. I know now why the Scripture says, "Two are better than one . . . because if one falls down, his friend can help him up . . . Though one may be overpowered, two can defend themselves." It is true that a cord of three strands is not easily broken, and you have been used by God to keep me from being broken on so many occasions. Thank you for passionately and tirelessly serving God by serving me. I know that your hands are raw from scrubbing carrots, and your body is weary from fighting alongside me . . . but I am so grateful. When I stop to think about what you have done for me in this past year, I know that I have encountered God in you. Thanks for all the times you've said "I want you to live!" I'd marry you all over again.

INTRODUCTION

Although the stories of our lives are different, the Pursuer of our hearts is passionately seeking to lead us all to one place—a place called Surrender. The pages of this book are the tale of one person's journey toward that place. They are written in the hope that you might be able to see His hand in your own story. Regardless of whether we are always aware of it or not, the Lover of Our Souls is pursuing us with reckless abandon, not to harm us or to demand obedience, but to give us a gift.

His voice is never silent, although few stop long enough to listen. He beckons us through the beauty of a sunset, or the splendor of a star-filled night sky. He calls to us in the delivery room as we see a baby take its first breath, or as the words of a worship tune echo in our mind. But the simple joys of this life are not His only mouthpiece. Sometimes His voice is most clearly heard in our greatest disappointments, in our seasons of deepest pain. C.S. Lewis once said,

"God whispers to us in our joy, and He shouts in our pain."

Regardless of how God speaks, the truth is that He is speaking. He is pursuing. Can you see Him? Do you recognize His voice in the midst of your joy as well as your pain? The gift He seeks to give is far greater than what we might ever imagine and it often comes in a package we didn't anticipate. It isn't the gift of blessings—a great job, good kids, more money, influential ministry, or close friends. It isn't the gift of a smoother life—fewer problems, fewer arguments, fewer defiant kids, or fewer months of unemployment. God's gift to us is the gift of Himself.

God is infinitely creative in the methods He employs to take our wandering eyes and rivet them on Himself. It's not that we prefer to disregard Him. Usually, we just don't see how badly we need Him, or understand the depth of the joy we will find when we encounter Him. You might say the story that follows is the story of how God got my undivided attention, and of the things I saw and heard once I began to look and listen more closely.

Dan Roelofs
September 2002

CHAPTER 1

RESTING IN HIS SHADOW

It is amazing how three simple words can change everything about how you see the world. On November 27th, 2001, there were several random thoughts floating through my mind. *I am once again 1500 miles past due on an oil change . . . I still need to follow up with a new couple I met at church on Sunday . . . I wonder what my son's kindergarten teacher will want to talk about at his parent/teacher conference. . . Minneapolis traffic is getting to be ridiculous. . .*

On November 28th, none of those issues had any significance whatsoever, for that day I heard three words I never dreamed would be spoken to me. "You have cancer." In a heartbeat, things that were once huge concerns were not concerns at all. At the same time, a whole new set of questions filled my mind. *How could this happen to me? I'm so healthy. What are my chances to survive? How long do I have to live? What am I going to say to my wife? I want to see my kids grow up! God, what are You doing, what are You saying, what's going on?*

Interestingly, the day before I was diagnosed, I was reading in the book of Jeremiah. I was struck by the pain, the hardship, and the apparent ineffectiveness of his ministry. I wrote in my journal:

Is it possible to experience what Jeremiah did and still be joyful and even satisfied? The real question is essentially, "Is God enough, or isn't He? Can God satisfy the deepest needs of my heart, or can He not?" Even if I had to experience pain like Jeremiah did, it would not affect my goal, nor the source of my life, my joy, and my satisfaction. Nothing in all creation can keep me from abiding in His love.

The verse I camped on that day was Jeremiah 20:11, "But the Lord is with me like a mighty warrior." Then came cancer.

A WHOLE NEW WORLD

I left the doctor's office on that particular Wednesday morning with instructions to be back at the hospital next door in a few hours for a CT scan.

It was evident that there was cancer in my lymph nodes, but we needed to find out where else it had spread. I drove out of the parking lot stunned. As I headed down the road, I looked at the people on the street. Some of them were elderly, and I wondered how they had survived such a cruel world for so long. *I don't smoke, I work out three times a week, and I don't even drink soda. How can this be happening in my body? It's one thing for someone who has abused their body their whole life to get sick—that makes sense to me. But this—this doesn't make sense.*

I called my wife, Tammy, as I drove. I didn't say the c-word. I told her I needed to have some tests later that day and then they would know more. "We can't know anything for sure until they've done the scans." I had already been told it was improbable that the lump under my arm was anything other than melanoma. Four years before, I'd had a mole removed from my chest that tested positive for melanoma, which is a form of skin cancer.

I had surgery and the doctor said, "There is a 95 percent chance you won't ever see this again. Don't worry about it." So we didn't. At least, I didn't. That's why I knew this had to be a mistake. I believed the five percent couldn't include me. *I have two little boys,* I thought to myself. *God just called me to start*

*a new church, we just moved into a new house . . .
this isn't adding up.*

I drove to the office of a close friend who is a
mortgage banker. After a closing on a house, he
and I were going to help some friends move. I told
him and his office partners what was going on, and
we got on the Internet—hoping, searching, and
desperately wanting to find some information that
would tell me this wasn't as serious as the doctor
was making it sound. Everything we found told me
the opposite. The most common word associated
with melanoma seemed to be "deadly." There were a
few references to "incurable." Everything I read was
discouraging—statistics, survival rates, medical
jargon about treatment and diagnosis—it was like a
whole new, terrifying world. Now it was my world,
a world I didn't want to live in or have any part of.

I went to the new home my friends were moving
into and did everything I could to appear cheery
and excited for them on their big day. Inside I wanted to scream. I wanted someone to tell me, "You
aren't going to die." At the moment, death was a
subject I couldn't get out of my mind.

After a couple hours of moving boxes, I drove
to Methodist Hospital, drinking the barium given
to me for the CT scan as I drove. I got to the hos-

pital early, so I took my briefcase into the waiting room with me. I thought about looking through my Palm Pilot to see what work was left to be done in the week, but I just didn't have the motivation. My to-do list seemed so meaningless at the moment. I pulled out my *One Year Bible* and started to read.

The *One Year Bible* is divided into daily readings that include a section from the Old Testament, one from the New Testament, a Psalm, and a Proverb for each day. The Psalm for the day was Psalm 90; it's a prayer of Moses, and one of its primary themes is the brevity of life. Verse 12 says, "Teach us to number our days aright that we might gain a heart of wisdom."

I had memorized that verse in college, and now its significance was so evident to me. No one knows how many days he has, yet I had always assumed there were many more years in store for me. The question, "What would I do differently if I could live my life again?" gripped me.

There was nothing super encouraging about Psalm 90:

"You turn men back to dust, saying, 'Return to dust, O sons of men.' For a thousand years in your sight are like a day that has just gone by, or like a watch in the night.

23

You sweep men away in the sleep of death; they are like the new grass of the morning— though in the morning it springs up new, by evening it is dry and withered . . . the length of our days is seventy years—or eighty if we have the strength; yet their span is but trouble and sorrow, for they quickly pass, and we fly away." (Psalm 90:3-6, 10)

The Psalm rang true in my heart, and yet it seemed too late to apply it to my own life. I thought of the times I could have paid more attention to my boys and didn't. The times I said yes to sin and no to God. The times I didn't stop to talk to my neighbor in his yard because I had important things to do. The times I chose to be busy instead of lingering in God's presence. The times I was unkind to my wife, and the times I let my work become more important than my relationship with her. The times I was too busy to enjoy my friends—to just enter into a conversation with no thoughts of the day's to-do list.

Why have I been so stinkin' busy?! What have I been striving for, clamoring after, grasping at? Is it worth it? Is it lasting? Is it even important? I wanted to go back and do it over again—loving God more than anything else in life. *If only I could live those years again, seeing each day the way I see them now,* I reflected.

Obviously, that luxury wasn't an option. I sat there in the waiting room with a heart full of regret. My life appeared to be coming to an end, and I was pretty sure God wasn't pleased with the way I had lived it. Fortunately, God led me to keep reading.

DO NOT FEAR

The next chapter in the book of Psalms, the 91st, had an entirely different message. I read the first verse and couldn't read any more. "He who dwells in the shelter of the Most High will rest in the shadow of the Almighty."

As I read it, my eyes filled with tears. Suddenly, it was very apparent that God was in the room with me. For a moment, time stood utterly still. I didn't hear a booming voice, but I knew that God had spoken to me through His Word. In the gentlest, kindest way He said, "Dan, I am here. I am with you. I want to give you rest. I will be with you on every step of this journey. Do not fear."

A heavy wave of emotion came over me. The possibility of internal rest seemed too good to be true. The thought that God loved me enough to want to give me this gift made me weep. Suddenly,

I realized where I was, and that people were looking at me as my eyes filled with tears. I wiped my face with my sleeve and tried to regain my composure. Then I went on reading.

"I will say of the Lord, 'He is my refuge and my fortress, my God in whom I trust.' Surely He will save you from the fowler's snare, and from the deadly pestilence. He will cover you with His feathers, and under His wings you will find refuge; His faithfulness will be your shield and rampart. You will not fear the terror of night, nor the arrow that flies by day, nor the pestilence that stalks in the darkness, nor the plague that destroys at midday. A thousand may fall at your side, ten thousand at your right hand, but it will not come near you. You will only observe with your eyes and see the punishment of the wicked. If you make the Most High your dwelling—even the Lord, who is my refuge—then no harm will befall you, no disaster will come near your tent. For He will command His angels concerning you to guard you in all your ways; they will lift you up in their hands so that you will not strike your foot against a stone. You will tread upon the lion and the cobra; you will trample the great lion and the serpent. 'Because he loves me,' says the Lord, 'I will rescue him; I will protect him for he acknowledges My name. He will call upon Me, and I will answer him; I will be with him in trouble, I will deliver him and honor him. With long life will I satisfy him and show him My salvation'" (Psalm 91:2-16)

In Philippians 4:7, Paul reminds us that there is a peace that comes from God that goes beyond human comprehension. It doesn't make sense. It defies logic. I had taught the students in my youth group that this peace was real, and we could trust God to grant it when we gave our burdens to Him in prayer. But I had never experienced such a dire need for it.

As I sat there in the waiting room, this peace enveloped me. Psalm 91 had just described all kinds of perilous situations, none of which were too great for the power and peace of God. And now He was proving it to me. This was encounter number one with the living, loving God since the journey with cancer had begun, and there would be many more to follow. I lay down on the CT scan table without fear. God was with me. What more did I need?

CHAPTER 2

PERFECT PEACE

Waking up the morning after being diagnosed was a strange experience. There was a part of me that thought it must all be a bad dream. However, the news of the day before was still a reality in my life, one that would change me forever. While God had given me peace, it didn't keep me from grieving.

I dropped my son off at kindergarten and drove to my favorite spot overlooking the lake near our house. I had met the Lord there on so many occasions before, and now it just seemed like the place where I needed to be. I parked my car and tried to collect my thoughts. As I started to pray, I was overwhelmed with grief. I sobbed and sobbed as I thought about leaving my boys and my wife behind. I didn't want to die. I could imagine the questions coming from my kids, "When is Daddy coming back? Why did he die? Who is going to tuck me in at night? Will we see Daddy in Heaven?"

As quickly as it started, it was over. The tears were like a refreshing spring rain. The pain inside me needed to come out, and when I poured out my heart to God, I was renewed. It felt so good to spill out the pain and angst and grief, and know that God understood and cared.

Thursday night my doctor called and confirmed what he had originally suspected. The tissue removed from my lymph node was indeed cancerous, and the scans showed that there were also small nodules in my left lung and liver. It wasn't quite clear whether these nodules were cancerous or not because they were too small to be classified as anything but "indiscriminant." He told me the only way we could know for sure what these were would be to have another scan in a month or so and compare them. If the spots had grown, they were cancer. If not, then it was probable that they were only cysts.

SHARING THE NEWS

Now that I had somewhat of a definitive answer about what we were facing, it was time to start sharing the news. I remember how excited I was to tell everyone when each of our boys was born—I couldn't wait to call everyone I knew! This time, it was the exact opposite. I knew my brother and sister and parents were going to be crushed, and telling them was going to be gut-wrenching.

I called my brother first. I did everything I could to tell him as matter-of-factly as possible. I put every positive spin I could on it, hoping not to cause any more pain or worry than I had to. Mark was brave on the phone. I found out later that he wept uncontrollably after we hung up.

Then I started to think about how to tell my parents. They were visiting my sister and brother-in-law in Louisville, and they had been looking forward to this weekend together for so long. I didn't want to ruin it by sharing bad news. I prayed, and God seemed to be leading me to tell them now, rather than waiting for them to come home. I did, and later they told me they were so glad. They were able to pray and cry together with my sister Rachel and her husband, and found a good deal of comfort in being able to walk through that part of the valley together.

After sharing with some close friends, the next hurdle to clear was telling our fledgling church.

It had been only two and a half months since our grand opening as a church, and now this. I poured my heart out to God. "What do I say, Lord? How do I tell this group of people in a way that will give You glory and keep them from worry or fear?" God led me back to Psalm 91. I decided to show them what God had shown me. The title of my message: "Perfect Peace."

The image in my mind that I wanted to share with our church family was that of the lake a block from our house. Usually on Sundays I would drive over to the movie theater where we met for worship and help set up the rooms early in the morning. Oftentimes at 7:00 a.m., the lake had a thin mist rising above it, and a perfect reflection, just as if it were a mirror of glass. Not a ripple in sight. That was a picture of what God had done in my heart. Instead of a raging sea, it was perfectly calm and undisturbed. I had no other explanation other than the fact that this peace was not my own—it was a gift from God. It was a morning of prayer and worship I will never forget.

According to the prophet Isaiah, we should not be surprised at this kind of peace. It is promised to those who fix their eyes on the Source of peace. Isaiah 26:3 says, "You will keep in perfect peace him whose mind is steadfast, because he trusts in You." What an incredible promise!

One of the nurses at the cancer center saw that there was something different in my eyes compared to what she saw in the eyes of so many others at the treatment center. "If only the other patients here could find that kind of peace," she said to me one day. I had already told her it was from God, but she didn't understand. It isn't for the religious, or those who have lived a perfect life. There is a peace and a rest that can't be earned or bought or contrived by any human. It is a gift one receives when he chooses to make the Lord his refuge and fortress, the God in whom he can trust.

TRUE SECURITY

People often equate security with peace of mind. I've had numerous insurance agents tell me that if I had more insurance, I'd have more peace of mind. Security is a term that defines something that cannot be taken away. To be insecure is to be worried that what you have can be taken away. When the Psalmist describes God as a refuge in Psalm 91:2, he is saying that God is the ultimate security—the ultimate in protection. To be in His presence is to be completely and totally safe, and that is what I was experiencing. He never leaves our presence, but we are often very unaware of His.

There are two things about God that make Him the ultimate protector. The first is that He is infinitely powerful. He is more powerful than anything else that could come against us. This is why, in His shadow, pestilence, sickness, and disaster have no power over us to cause us to fear.

Secondly, He is loving. If my heavenly dad doesn't love me, I don't care if He is the strongest, richest guy in the world. Why? It is His love that brings His power and His riches to my aid. How do I know He will use what He has to help me unless I am assured that He is in love with me?

The image in verse 4 of Psalm 91 points toward the love of our Protector. "He will cover you with His feathers, and under His wings you will find refuge; His faithfulness will be your shield and rampart." The picture is that of a mother hen. Danger is approaching, but she will give up her life before she lets her little ones be harmed, so she pulls them close with a sweep of her wing and covers them. Under those wings, the chicks are safe. It is the love of our Heavenly Father that causes Him to use all of His power and might to protect us.

In verse 11, the Psalmist says God even dispatches His angels, mighty heavenly beings that are at His command, to protect us. They are sent to "guard us in all our ways." There is no path I could take where I would be forgotten. There was no place I could go where I would be out of God's sight. There was no challenge in my life that would somehow slip through without His notice.

I don't know that there was ever a time before where God used a passage so personally and powerfully in my life. He was equipping me to fight the battle He knew was ahead.

On November 29, the day after being diagnosed, I read Psalm 94:17-19, "Unless the Lord had given me help, I would soon have dwelt in the silence of death. When I said, 'My foot is slipping,' Your love, O Lord, supported me. When anxiety was deep within me, Your consolation brought joy to my soul."

I journaled my response:

I got the lab report back yesterday and the tissue in my lymph node was cancerous. All props are gone. I am in a situation where I can totally and completely throw myself upon God. He is the only One who can sustain me and He will sustain me. His love is my support, and His consolation my joy. The words of the song

"Deep, Deep Love of Jesus" call His love "vast, unmeasured, boundless, and free." It is this love that encourages me, protects me, surrounds me, and gives my life meaning. It is this love that brings good out of every circumstance. It makes my life significant, it fills me up, it revives me, comforts me. It is the deep, deep love of Jesus that makes me sing and gives me joy. There is nothing else in all creation that compares to it. "Lord, I put my hope in Your love." Amen.

He has yet to disappoint me.

CHAPTER 3

A BATTLE TO FIGHT

While God made His peace readily available to me, it became evident after a short while that I had a role to play in letting this peace reign in me. There was a battle to fight and it took place in my mind. It would have been challenging enough had it been purely a physical battle. But Scripture makes it clear that the battle for the mind is a spiritual one.

The Apostle Paul wrote to the Corinthians about this battle:

> "For though we live in the world, we do not wage war as the world does. The weapons we fight with are not the weapons of the world. On the contrary, they have divine power to demolish strongholds. We demolish arguments and every pretension that sets itself up

against the knowledge of God, and we take captive every thought to make it obedient to Christ." (2 Corinthians 10:3-5)

Satan is a deceiver, and the father of lies (John 8:44). More than ever before, I was conscious of the spiritual battle going on in me and around me. Even though I knew the truth taught in Psalm 91, I had to use it, or fear was right around the corner. I felt weak at a time when I desperately wanted to be strong—not only for myself but for my wife, my kids, and those I was responsible to lead. My December 2nd journal entry gives evidence of this:

Lord, I couldn't meet my needs before and I sure can't today. All I can do is trust that You know what You are doing, and that to be in Your arms, in the palm of Your hand, is the best place I could ever be. I need to know You today like I've never known You before. Grant me the gift of faith. I need Your encouragement, I need to hear Your voice, I simply need You—everything that You are. Please Lord!

Help me to fight today, Lord. Help me to win the battle that takes place in my mind. Help me to not give in to fear. Make my faith strong. Help me to focus on Your truth, not on Satan's lies. Help me to rejoice in You in ways

*I never have before. Help me to celebrate You,
to cherish You, to savor You, to bank on You.
I want to know what it really means to trust
You, to truly walk by faith.*

One of the first places this battle would be fought was regarding whether we could truly trust God to lead us as we made decisions about my cancer treatment. There were myriad possible choices in front of us. Everything in my gut told me I needed to worry that if we made the wrong decision, it would cost me my life.

I had given counsel to so many students in the past about trusting God to show them where to go to college, or whether to break up with their girlfriend, or which job to take. I had always believed that God could be trusted to lead us if we put our faith in Him. Suddenly I was questioning the validity of all those promises in Scripture. It made sense in my head that I should leave this in God's hands, and yet inside I desperately wanted to take control. Nonetheless, God continued to affirm His love for us, and His willingness to guide us through the words of Scripture.

Proverbs 3:5-6 says, "Trust in the Lord with all your heart, and lean not on your own understanding. In all your ways acknowledge Him, and He will make your paths straight."

Psalm 73: 23-24 says, "Yet I am always with You; You hold me by my right hand. You guide me with Your counsel and afterward You will take me into glory."

Psalm 32:8 says, "I will instruct you and teach you in the way you should go; I will counsel you and watch over you."

There was one affirmation after another in Scripture of the Lord's promise to guide us. The choice to trust Him was a daily one.

OUR WEAPONS: PRAYER AND SCRIPTURE

High on the list of priorities was to start sharing our needs with people who could pray for us. I needed prayer and I wanted a lot of it! Tammy and I got on the phone and started calling the friends we knew were prayer warriors.

One of the most meaningful times of prayer I had early in the battle was with the pastors and business leaders in Elk River, the city where I pastored. We shared an unusual unity and love for each other, a by-product of the times of prayer we shared together over the noon hour every Tuesday.

I shared my need with them, and they poured their hearts out before God on my behalf. That weekly hour of prayer was another encounter with God that won't be forgotten. Some quietly petitioned God for my life, while others literally cried out to God, asking Him to destroy the cancer and heal me for the glory of His name. This outpouring of love and concern from so many people on our behalf was truly from God, His love being demonstrated through His body, the Church.

It was very humbling to see men so unselfishly concerned for me. I felt very unworthy. But God spoke softly and powerfully to me through these men, saying, "You are worth fighting for. You are worth the prayers, the tears, the concern. I love you."

Scripture that I had memorized or studied years earlier became precious to me as each day Tammy and I fought for my life and our joy. So many passages that were once simply words on a page started to come to life. We learned that the Bible really was a sword in our hand, and it became our primary defense against every flaming arrow of doubt and fear and discouragement. What was so amazing, even to a guy people call Pastor, was the power and the victory we experienced when we used the Word of God. As Tammy said, "Scripture just plain works!"

Tammy was battling right alongside me, and I saw her grow even more in her love for God and

His Word. She took several spiritual warfare verses and other verses speaking the promises of God and taped them to the window above the kitchen sink. We knew we had to do everything we could to fill our minds with the truth that could set us free.

One day, I was lying inside an MRI machine while they looked for evidences of cancer on my brain and liver. Just the sight of the equipment (the long narrow tube), and the thought of what the tests might turn up, tempted me to become fearful. My friend Paul had already prepped me for the whole experience by saying, "Close your eyes before you go into the tube and don't open them, no matter what happens! Pretend you're on the beach. If you open your eyes, you're done for! The claustrophobia will take over!"

As the machine made its gruesome noises and I was trying to lie still, I realized I had a choice as to what I could think about. I started to praise God right there in the tube with the words of Psalm 100: "Shout for joy to the Lord, all the earth. Worship the Lord with gladness; come before Him with joyful songs." The words of Psalm 46 also came to mind: "God is our refuge and our strength, an ever-present help in trouble. Therefore, we will not fear, though the earth give way and the mountains fall into the heart of the sea." Verse 5 says, *"God is within her, she will not fall."*

Confidence in the purposes of God began to well up inside me. As I meditated on the greatness and glory of God, I began to feel invincible in Christ. That night I wrote in my journal:

> *Life and death are not in my hands, but victory is my birthright in Christ. Jesus bought it for me! I do not have to cave in to selfishness or fear or depression. These are all tools of Satan. God defeated him on the cross of Christ, and His victory is mine!*

> *I will not just survive, I will do it triumphantly, just like Jesus. There is great joy that God has in store for me—joy that is greater than any earthly pleasure. God is taking away my earthly dependencies in order to give me Himself. What an unbelievable gift!*

CHAPTER 4

JOY IN SUFFERING

The first recommendation from both of the doctors I met with regarding my case was to surgically remove the cancerous mass of lymph nodes. The surgery date was set for December 11th. Tammy, her dad, and I drove down to Fairview Riverside Hospital early in the morning to get registered for the surgery. After getting checked in, we had time to spend while I waited for my turn to be wheeled away on a gurney into the OR. I pulled out my Bible and turned to Psalm 68; verses 19 and 20 jumped out at me: "Praise be to God, our Savior, who daily bears our burdens. Our God is a God who saves; from the Sovereign Lord comes escape from death."

God reassured me that I was not entering surgery alone. Whatever burden I was carrying in regard to the outcome, I certainly didn't need to carry, because God wanted to take it on His shoulders. I wrote in my journal the next morning:

It is an amazing privilege to have the God of the universe so intimately involved in my life that He would care to bear my burdens. Father, You are amazing. You are a wonderful, powerful Savior. I love You. Once again I surrender my life to You. Use it to point people to You, for Your glory.

As we waited for the nurse to call my name, others came to wait with us and to be with us through the surgery. My mentor, a pastor I had worked with in a previous church, Tammy's brother, sister, and brother-in-law were all there. The group filled up the entire waiting room! Someone accused us of having more fun than we should have been having at 7:00 a.m. in a hospital waiting room.

After I had been prepped and was lying on the gurney, they came in to pray for me. My dad's cousin, Gary Roelofs, who had also been a mentor to me for the last few years, led the prayer time. There is never a really good time to pray before surgery as far as the doctors and nurses are concerned— they want to keep things moving and on schedule. However, when Gary began to pray, the nurses who came in stopped in their tracks and stood around the outside of the circle.

As Gary prayed a passionate prayer, entrusting me to God, he broke down with emotion. The warmth of God's presence filled the room, and any anxiety I had brought into the room with me completely vanished. I looked up at the attending nurse when Gary finished, and it was obvious she was moved by what she had just observed. As I was wheeled into surgery, I felt deeply loved by the friends and family who had come, and even more loved by my heavenly Father.

The surgery went well, and I came out of the recovery stage effortlessly. I'd previously felt anxiety when coming out of the anesthesia after other procedures, but that was not the case this time. I was completely at ease. They brought me back to the room and the party continued. More friends, more family, and a spirit of joy filled the air. I can't explain why except for the fact that God had made it very clear to all of us that He was firmly in control, and His plans are good. (That, of course, and the fact that the drugs were making me say some really funny stuff. I wondered later why all of my best lines are said when I'm not in my right mind.)

TREATMENT

Surgery was the first step toward eradicating the cancer in my body, and treatment would be the next. After praying a great deal and doing hours of Internet research, we decided to go to a cancer treatment facility in Illinois. We felt good about the fact that they combined traditional oncology with diet and naturopathic medicine. They seemed to offer a very balanced approach to treating cancer. We booked our flights, arranged for Tammy's family to take care of our boys, and left to begin treatment on January 2nd.

The next month of my life was the most difficult one that I had ever experienced. The treatment consisted of two drugs that were classified as immunotherapy. The goal of immunotherapy is not to kill the cancer, but to stimulate the patient's own immune system to fight the irregular cells. The drugs were Interleukin 2 and Interferon. Each round of treatment started on Monday night and finished five days later, with a week of recuperation in between. The drugs were given intravenously, and their effects were high fevers, uncontrollable chills and shaking, vomiting and dry heaving, water retention, irregular heartbeat, hives, mouth sores, and loss of appetite.

There were many times in the midst of a weekly treatment that I simply wanted to die. I just wanted an end to the misery. I lost my motivation to get well, I lost my love for everything good, and my desires were narrowed down to one thing: getting rid of the pain. God seemed a million miles away. Any feeble attempts to worship or pray or read Scripture were met with confusion in my mind, hopelessness, and despair. In addition to this, Satan seemed to be attacking our church in some not-so-subtle ways. I was at the end of my rope.

In between treatments, I was reading a book written by John Piper called *The Swan Is Not Silent.* It describes the lives of three men who suffered greatly, but in their suffering saw God greatly glorified. In a chapter about a man named John Bunyan, there was a line that grabbed me. Piper wrote that, based on his observation of Bunyan's life and the lives of other saints through the centuries, there is more of God to be had during suffering than any other time in life. My attention was directed to Job, who said after suffering, "My ears had heard of you, but now my eyes have seen you." Incredible! Suffering could be the vehicle in my life to take me from hearing of God to truly seeing Him. The wind of the Spirit was breathing life into my soul again.

The next day I recorded the following in my journal:

Cancer would seem like an incredible waste if there were not more of God to be had through it. As it is, the things of this world are looking less and less attractive. I have an insatiable hunger for God—to see more of Him, to experience more of His love, more of His power, more of His blessing. I want to be in the middle of what He is doing—to have a life, a marriage, a family, and a ministry that are blessed by Him, marked by His presence and power. I am so helpless to bring this about, but according to Psalm 91 and Psalm 116, all I need to do is simply call on Him. This is the solution to every challenge, every difficulty, every trial, and every problem.

GOD'S LOVE MADE REAL

This change of perspective was not the only miracle God did during that period of time. There was another valuable lesson He wanted to teach me, and that is how to receive.

Being a pastor, I am well acquainted with the joy that is found in giving. I knew the satisfaction that came with helping to meet a need in someone's life—especially as it pertained to one's spiritual life. But being in the midst of a brutal treatment put me in the position of being the one in a place of need. I had never before needed supportive people around me quite as much as I did then. When I was finding it impossible to connect with God, when I was questioning where God was, when I couldn't see Him or touch Him or even keep my thoughts focused on Him for more than a moment, God walked into the room in the form of a friend.

One friend named Clark dropped everything at a moment's notice, got into his car, and drove to Illinois so he could be next to my bed when I began treatment. There was compassion in his eyes as he cleaned up the vomit at my bedside.

My close friend and accountability partner, Ross, decided to fly in from South Carolina to spend four days next to my bed. He laid ice packs on my head to help me deal with the fever. He went for more blankets, he prayed over me, he pressed the doctors for information, he dressed me, and he served me in every way for four days.

Jo made a photo stand with pictures of my boys to put at the end of my bed so I would fight to live when I saw their faces. Tammy's family put their plans aside so they could take care of our boys. My parents made the five-hour trip to be with us each weekend in between treatments, and my mother took a week off from work to help us around the house. Several friends told me they were ready to get on a plane at any moment and fly to Chicago if I told them I wanted them next to the bed.

Randee cooked special meals for me. Caryn became a personal nurse to me in between treatments. Rich and Paul fixed my cars. Groups of people brought meals, babysat our kids, painted walls in our house, and bought airline tickets for Tammy to be able to join me at the hospital. The list goes on. At the top of this list, however, was my wife Tammy. She was dying inside as she watched me lie there in pain, but served me in countless ways every day in spite of it.

There comes a time when failing to receive is nothing less than pride and arrogance. God was showing me that to be weak is not necessarily a bad thing. It paved the way for me to experience His love in a way that I never would have expected it— through the people with whom He had surrounded me. In 1 John 4:12 we read, "No one has ever seen God, but when we love one another God lives in us and His love is made complete in us." Because I was weak, I had the privilege of seeing God through the love of people. It was a rare gift, and one I appreciated dearly.

CHAPTER 5

THE DARKEST NIGHT

February 4th, 2002, was the first day of round three of my immunotherapy treatment. I wondered whether my body could survive another round, but I knew God was with me, and just knowing that kept my fears at bay. I had flown to the treatment center by myself on Sunday evening and spent the night across the street from the hospital in one of their residences. Tammy was planning to join me at the hospital on Monday, and she was flying with my mentor, Gary, who had volunteered to spend some time at our side while I entered this crucial phase of treatment.

Typically, the doctors would give four rounds of the treatment and then have the patient scanned to see how effective the treatment had been before making further decisions about what to do next. For some reason, I was able to talk my doctor into authorizing a scan after two rounds of treatment. The scan took place Monday afternoon; afterwards I prepared to get checked into a hospital room so that treatment could begin.

DEVASTATING NEWS

While Gary, Tammy, and I were sitting in the waiting room, my doctor came in and motioned for me to come with him. I assumed it was to authorize the start of round three and direct me to the nurse who would get me situated in a room. Instead, he took me to his office. He shut the door and as he looked at some papers on his desk he said, "Well, the scan didn't show what we were hoping for." My mind raced. First of all, I had no idea the scan results would be available so soon. *What was he telling me? What did this mean?*

He continued, "The tumors on your lungs, that we measured a month ago, have all grown, and it appears there are several new nodules on both lungs." For a minute, I couldn't even grasp what he was saying. When my pulse slowed a little and my mind cleared, I began asking questions.

"What are my options? Do I have to continue

with this treatment? Is this evidence that this treatment is totally ineffective for me, or is there sometimes a delayed reaction in the immune system?" The conversation closed with him telling me that he wanted to talk to a couple of other melanoma specialists overnight and meet with me again the next day. I shut the door behind me and went back to tell Tammy and Gary what I'd just found out.

I have never seen a more painful look in my wife's eyes. Had we not been in a waiting room, she probably would have screamed, or wept, but somehow she fought back the tears and asked, "What do we do now?" We went down to the cafeteria and tried to eat. Tammy started making phone calls. I don't know how she did it. I couldn't talk to anyone during that time.

Gary just stayed close. He didn't give advice or try to fix things, thankfully, but I knew he was hurting right along with us. He was simply applying Romans 12:15: "Rejoice with those who rejoice; mourn with those who mourn." It was just what we needed.

Eventually we walked back to the cottage where we were staying and sat down in the living room. I didn't know what to say, what to do. For a while we just sat in silence. I pulled out my journal and began to pour my heart out to God.

Lord, You know I've experienced every emotion under the sun in the last few hours. "Whom have I in heaven but You, and earth has nothing I desire besides You. My flesh and my heart may fail, but God is the strength of my heart and my portion forever" (Psalm 73:25-26). I have no strength of my own right now, but You are my strength. You are my security, my protector, and my healer. I give You my broken body and ask You to make me whole. I give You my heart and ask You to give me the grace to keep trusting, to keep believing You, to keep resting in Your care, to keep loving You with everything in me. Just keep me close to You, Jesus. If there were ever a time when I needed to hear Your voice, it is now. Lead me by the hand.

Protect Tammy and her heart. Give her grace to trust. I pray the same for Mark and Rachel and Mom and Dad, and anyone else who might be struggling because of this. Thank You for making me Your child. I am Yours, Lord.

After several minutes, Ross called and offered to pray with me. I remember that God gave him amazing perspective as he prayed—especially since I knew he was hurting, too. He led me to worship God—not because God always does what I want, but because He is Lord; He is good, He is loving, and He is wise. Regardless of what I might have thought about God at that moment, I knew that what Ross prayed was true, and I wanted to worship.

When we finished, I lay down on our bed, exhausted. I wanted to get away from the pain of all the despairing thoughts that were filling my mind. As I struggled to drift off to sleep, my mind raced with thoughts about my funeral. I pictured my boys growing up without me, and I grieved the pain I knew Tammy would suffer. Death didn't seem like such a bad thing for me, but my heart was breaking for them.

Why, God? Is this how You treat those who love You? I've served You faithfully and this is my reward? Where are You? What are You doing? I don't want to die, Jesus. I love my boys so much. I love my wife. I can't leave Tammy all alone. What about the church? Are You going to allow Satan to destroy what You just started to build? The words of the Psalmist, David, came to mind. "How can a man praise You if he is dead? How can I give You glory from the

59

grave?" *It was the darkest night my soul had ever known.*

Isaiah 50 is a passage that speaks about life in the dark. Verse 10 reads, "Who among you fears the Lord and obeys the word of His servant? Let him who walks in darkness, who has no light, trust in the name of the Lord and rely on his God."

In the mid-nineties, Tammy and I did an internship with Dr. Neil Anderson and Freedom In Christ Ministries. On several occasions, Neil shared about how God had used that passage to bring him through a time of darkness in his life. I remembered Neil saying, "The night is always darkest just before the dawn." I knew the Bible answer for what I was facing. It just seemed so difficult to get my arms around it at the moment.

Eventually, mercifully, God allowed me to drift off to sleep. I woke up several times during the night, and just like that, thoughts of death were right in my face. It seemed like a nightmare from which I couldn't wake up.

CHAPTER 6

IT'S NOT ABOUT CANCER

"Dan, you need to go talk to Pam!" Tammy exclaimed. "She has a message for us, and I think you'll really be encouraged." Pam was another melanoma patient we had gotten to know in the hospital. She was receiving the same treatment I had undergone. She was a petite little gal, and a fiery believer. She was a Christian spark plug if I've ever seen one! We really enjoyed getting to know her and her husband, Vince.

Tammy had gone to see how she was doing while I slept in the morning after the bad news came. I had no idea what Pam had said to Tammy, but there was something different in my wife's countenance. She had gone to bed fearful and depressed, just like I did, but that is not what I saw on her face now.

After meeting with my doctor, Tammy and I went back to Pam's room so I could hear whatever she wanted to tell us. Pam's room was dark. The shades were pulled so that if her discomfort ever lessened, she was able to grab brief snatches of restful sleep. The room was divided in half by a curtain, with another patient on the other side. We made our way over to the side of her bed, and her face perked up when she saw us. She was sweating with fever and had ice packs resting on a damp cloth on her forehead. "I wanted Dan to hear your perspective on our situation, too, Pam," Tammy whispered. "Do you mind?"

"I'm so glad you came," Pam said with as strong a voice as she could muster. "I really think you are in the midst of a spiritual battle." She held her hand up with her thumb and forefinger an inch apart and said, "You are this close to entering into the Promised Land. You can't give up now. Satan wants you to focus on the giants and the obstacles."

Suddenly, a voice from the other side of the curtain boomed, "And he's a liar!" It was Pam's roommate, a very sweet woman who also happened to be a believer. We all laughed for a minute when we realized she'd been listening to our conversation. Then we turned our attention back to Pam.

"God isn't done with you yet, Dan. He has work for you to do. Satan knows the lives you'll touch. Don't let him make you fear. Don't let him! Focus on the Lord. Focus on the Promised Land!" At this point, I could tell Pam was exhausting herself by simply talking. Tammy and I gave her a squeeze on the hand, thanked her, and told her we promised to keep in touch. We left her room, never to see her on Earth again. She walked into the arms of Jesus two weeks later.

Whether Pam's message was truly a word from God, I don't know. I did not assume upon hearing it that God had just told me I would live and not die. However, there was much in what she said that was backed up in Scripture. I was reminded of the truth that fear and discouragement are never from God. I could choose my thoughts, and I left the conversation rejoicing inside that there is always hope with God, because He is bigger than any obstacle.

"We can't help you here anymore," my doctor had said to me that day. He suggested that I not continue on the Interferon and Interleukin because it was apparent they were not achieving any kind of immune response. He gave us a list of three or four websites, in order to look into treatments I might be able to receive elsewhere. "Good bye, and good luck," he said to us.

As we walked out of the hospital into the crisp February air, I turned around and said, "Good riddance." My memories of the treatment made me want to leave and never come back. Already, one prayer from the night before had been answered. I didn't know whether we would be offered more options at this treatment center, and I had asked God to clearly show us whether we were to continue here or not. When the doctor told us we couldn't be helped there anymore, that door was closed. There was no doubt. I left with a spring in my step and hope in my heart that somehow, God would make a way even when there seemed to be no way.

We got in the hospital limousine and rode back to the airport. Our plan was to stay overnight at an airport hotel and leave on the earliest flight the following morning. Gary had arranged for our flights to be changed at no charge by pulling some strings with a reservations manager at Northwest. It was not by chance that he had decided to come and be with us on this particular week. Tammy and I felt like little kids in a time of need, and he was like a strong parent when we needed someone to be strong for us.

We checked into the hotel, and I went down to arrange for a shuttle to bring us to the airport the following morning. When I came back to the room, I saw a sight I'll never forget. My wife was jumping on the bed. I couldn't help but stand there and laugh. It looked absolutely hilarious! It was just another piece of evidence to me that God was working in her heart to free her from fear and give her joy. Seeing that made it so much easier for me to trust God.

ANOTHER GOD ENCOUNTER

After a wonderful candlelit meal in the hotel restaurant, we came back to our room and plopped on the bed, exhausted. It had been a long and emotional day. We decided there was no better way to end it than by pouring out our hearts to God in prayer, together.

As Tammy prayed, I could tell her heart was full of gratitude. She thanked God for bringing my miserable treatment to an end. She thanked Him for allowing me to be scanned a month prior to when they would normally scan again. She thanked Him for arranging for Gary to be with us when we really needed someone there, for arranging our flights so we could go home, for all the people He had burdened to pray for us, and for the message of encouragement from Pam. On and on her list went.

My perspective was changing even while I listened to her pray. I started to understand just how kind God had been to us in all of this, and how much He had demonstrated His love and compassion and His commitment to provide for us. Then He began to whisper to my heart as I prayed for Him to show us what to do next. Much like the moment in the waiting room of the hospital, there were no audible voices, but I knew God was speaking.

This isn't about cancer. It never has been. It is about your heart. It is an opportunity for you to know Me in a way you have never known Me before. Don't worry about what to do next. I'll take care of that. I don't want you to focus on finding the right treatment. I want you to focus on Me—loving Me with everything in you.

I feel weird even writing those words. It seems so mystical. How could I know that this was God? All I can say is that, at the moment, there was no question in my mind as to who was speaking to me, and what He was saying. I would have had reason to question it if it did not line up with Scripture, because God never contradicts His Word. But there is ample Scripture to back up the message God had just spoken personally to me, the primary passage being Matthew 6:31-33:

"So do not worry saying 'What shall we eat?' or 'What shall we drink?' or 'What shall we wear?' For the pagans run after all these things and your heavenly Father knows that you need them. But seek first His kingdom and His righteousness and all these things will be given to you as well."

I realized that oftentimes when confronted with problems or challenges, I have seen the problem as something to solve, something to get rid of. I have spent much of my life investing time and energy into creating a smoother path or a more problem-free life. My prayers have usually been something like, "God, take this away. God, heal this. Why won't You remove this obstacle in front of me? What is the solution to this problem?"

God seemed to be showing me that I was praying self-centered prayers and asking the wrong questions. Instead of seeing problems as bad and something to avoid at all costs, He wanted me to see His hand in them. Instead of asking Him to take them away, I needed to ask Him to open my eyes to what He wanted to show me through the challenge in front of me.

It became obvious to me on this day that cancer was not my greatest enemy. My greatest foe was anything that would keep me from living in intimacy with the Lord. The unbelief, the lack of trust, the self-sufficiency, the unsurrendered fears, the self-centered habits and patterns of thinking—these were the things God wanted to deal with. Cancer simply seemed to be a tool in His hand to cause me to stop and listen to Him, to really listen to Him. In that sense, it was an incredible blessing from God.

Before drifting off to sleep, I said, "Tammy, could you find a babysitter for the boys on Thursday?"

"Sure," she replied. "Why?"

"We're going to Timber Bay to listen to God."

Timber Bay is a camp and retreat center a couple hours north of us. It is a picturesque setting where I had often gone to have private prayer retreats. So many big life decisions were made in the quietness of a cabin or the stillness of the big woods there. And now, it seemed like the only reasonable thing to do next—get away to a quiet place where God could speak to us about our hearts. I was tempted to go there to demand that He talk to us about the next step, but I sensed He had something more personal, more powerful, to give us.

CHAPTER 7

A GOD-SIZED OPPORTUNITY

Thursday was not only the day we had set aside to pray and seek the Lord. It was also the day that a group of people at our former church had set aside to have a 24-hour prayer vigil for us. They had set it up believing I would be entering the most difficult period of the treatment on that day. It was incredibly humbling to think there would be an army of prayer warriors interceding on our behalf on this day. Before we left for the retreat center, I wanted to give them an update, and I sent out this e-mail:

Hello friends,

It is Thursday morning, and I wanted to send you an update because I realize many of you are focusing prayer on our behalf today.

69

I am humbled and honored and so incredibly grateful for your prayers. I just wonder what is going to happen in the heavenly realm today!

We are at home again because we found out on Tuesday that the treatment I was receiving was not effective in my case. It is apparent that the tumors have continued to grow unhindered. Since the treatment was so brutal, my doctor didn't see any point in doing two more rounds of therapy with no evidence at all that it was slowing any tumor growth. Tammy asked him, "Are you telling us we are done here?"

His answer was, "Yes." We were thankful God made this clear, because we have been praying for clarity as to what to do next, and that eliminates one thing from our list. Now we will seek the Lord about other treatment options. Everything regarding melanoma is experimental in that nothing has been really proven to work consistently, so our next step is a very significant decision.

We were very discouraged on Monday night after hearing the scan results. But God has since righted our ship and we now see it as a blessing and a redirection. The blessing is that we didn't go through four treatments before the scan, as normally is the case. We now have saved three weeks to do additional research and pray about pursuing another course of action.

God seems to be doing a unique thing in our hearts as well—giving us a strange confidence that He is in control and that our next steps will be clearly ordered by Him. Loving Him is truly all that matters right now. It may seem like this battle is about cancer and beating it and finding the right doctor or treatment plan, but God has made it clear that it is about our hearts, loving Him, and listening to His voice. The word "opportunity" keeps coming to mind, and that is what this is: an opportunity to know God in a way we never even dreamed possible before. With that, here are a few requests:

1. *Many of you have prayed for God's protection from severe side effects this week, and guess what—I haven't had any!*

2. *Praise God for sparing me from two more weeks of treatment. It was very much of Him that we found out it was ineffective when we did.*

3. *Please pray that God would show Tammy and me what it means to love Him with everything in us, in order that we*

71

would be able to surrender absolutely everything about our lives to Him and then be able to rest in this sweet surrender.

4. Pray that we would receive wisdom from God (James 1:5) and that our ears would hear a voice behind us saying, "This is the way, walk in it" (Isaiah 30:21).

5. Pray that God would continue to keep us focused on the Promised Land, and not on the giants (the tumors). We need to walk by faith, not be controlled by fear. Pray that all who are involved in this situation would stand on the Word of God and refuse to give in to the lies of our stinking, deceiving, lying, dirty, and rotten enemy. He has been defeated, and there is no way he is going to have the last word in this deal!

6. Pray that God would protect our boys, Taylor and Reid. They have had a challenging month, and are doing well. We simply want to pray God's protection for them and their spirits.

Thank you, thank you, thank you for praying! We love you and are honored to have you for friends. Your kindness to us is seen by the

*Lord, and is precious to Him. May God bless
you a ton today.*

Dan and Tammy

Our day at Timber Bay turned out to be one of
the greatest days in the life of our marriage. We
prayed together, listened to God together, and
laughed together. God did have much to say, and
none of it was about cancer treatment. He spoke to
us about our fears. He spoke to us about His perspective on our lives. More than anything else, He
used Scripture to reveal areas in our heart that were
keeping us from absolute surrender to Him. The
by-product of all these things was joy. We got in the
car to drive home full of gratitude for all God was
doing to draw us closer to Him.

God was giving us a peace in knowing that He
would be the One to lead us. The pressure was off!
We could trust that our steps would be ordered by
Him. I was reminded of a beautiful verse in Isaiah
58:11:

"The Lord will guide you always; He will
satisfy your needs in a sun-scorched land and
will strengthen your frame. You will be like a
well-watered garden, like a spring whose waters never fail."

CHAPTER 8

BELIEVING IS NOT SEEING

Knowing and believing that God would guide us, we also recognized that it is hard to steer a ship that isn't moving. We set out to find out everything we could about melanoma and the various methods being used to treat it. Someone had recommended we find a doctor who could be a "quarterback" for us. We needed someone who could see the whole field and understand what was going on well enough to guide us toward some viable options.

In the first week of pursuing leads, there were three different sources that recommended the same person. None of these people knew each other. It seemed as if God was surely heading us in that direction.

The oncologist recommended to us was known

as the best melanoma expert in the state of Minnesota. We booked an appointment with him for February 20th, which was two weeks away but the soonest we could get in. Two weeks seemed like an eternity, knowing that the cancer had been spreading like wildfire. However, God kept reminding us that His timing is perfect, and we had no reason to fear.

A CLOSED DOOR

February 20th was a gray, snowy day, and it matched what was going on in my heart as we drove down to the doctor's office. I remember walking up to the building and praying silently, *Lord, please let this man offer us some hope.* Suddenly, fear seemed to be knocking on the door again, when I had been so full of peace for the past several weeks. Being in the office was depressing. There were many chemo patients waiting for their treatment to start. *These people are dying,* I thought as I looked at them. Each one of them looked as if the flame of their hope had been snuffed out entirely.

Finally, our turn came and the nurse called us back. After doing a physical examination, the doctor appeared fairly surprised that I looked as healthy as I did, considering the fact that the cancer in my body was so advanced. The next part of the conversation is burned in my memory. The doctor outlined three potential options: the first option was chemotherapy and Interleukin, the second was a fairly untried vaccine, and the third was to do no treatment and enjoy life as long as I could while taking medication for the pain that was soon to arrive.

His next comment stopped me cold: "Mr. and Mrs. Roelofs, you need to understand that none of these treatments can be expected to be curative. With the disease at the stage it is in your body, all we can do is try to buy you some time. Our goal is to extend your life by as many days as we can and keep your pain at bay so that you can enjoy the time you have with your family."

"Buy us time?!" I had absolutely no interest in looking into options that would help to give me another month or two of life. The door I was praying would stay open had just been slammed shut. The hope I so longed for had not been offered. We got back in the car and headed for home.

The last time we received bad news, I was destroyed by it and God gave Tammy strength to support me. This time, I knew God wanted me to support her. She cried desperate tears. She screamed. She vented to God. Everything she was feeling and fearing and hoping for came out in a passionate burst of emotion as we made the lonely drive home. When she was finished, she put her head on my chest and we both cried in silence for the rest of the drive. I wasn't crying because I felt hopeless or angry. For some reason I still felt very confident that God was present with us, leading us. I cried because I have never seen anyone I love in that much pain, and it hurt me deeply.

Later in the day, I poured out my heart to God in my journal.

Father, You've promised me in Your Word that he who dwells in the shelter of the Most High will rest in the shadow of the Almighty. Your Word tells me You are my refuge. I have no other refuge but You. I want to live with everything in me. I want to disciple my boys. I want to grow old with Tammy. I can't bear the thought of coming Home right now. It is too painful. I need You, God. I feel like I've lost my perspective today, and I need Your help. Hold me, Lord. I can't do this without You. I need to hear Your voice.

NO REST WITHOUT SURRENDER

God answered my prayer and spoke to me through a message from Chuck Swindoll I heard on the radio. Years earlier, when I was 14, God used words that Swindoll had shared at a camp my family was attending in Mount Hermon, California, to draw me to Himself. I walked away from one of the meetings thinking to myself, *This God thing is for real, and I want Him in my life.* Now, 18 years later, God was speaking to me through him again. The message was called, "The Triumph of Trust." It was about Abraham and Isaac and what it meant to live with empty hands—holding nothing back from the Lord. My journal reflects the battle that was going on inside me:

> *I feel much like Abraham right now. It makes no sense to me why God would have me climbing the mountain with Isaac and a knife. Isaac was Abraham's most cherished treasure. In one sense, I guess my life is my cherished treasure. Abraham was led into the ultimate test of surrender, and that is where I believe I am now. I sense God asking me if I am willing to trust completely, to let go of every cherished desire in order to let Him give me what He wants to in return. There is no rest without surrender.*

I certainly did not want to surrender my life to God. At least, that is what my mind told me. But in my heart, I knew God wanted to free me of the burden of being in control of my own life. "Is God really good and is He truly loving?" is a question I struggled with daily at that point in my life. I knew I was supposed to believe that He is, but unless this truth reached my gut, unless I believed it in the deepest parts of me, I could not surrender. I could not rest in His arms. C.S. Lewis once wrote, "We don't doubt that God has His best in store for us; we fear how painful His best might be." This is exactly where I was.

God, in His kind and gentle way, reminded me that the truth about Himself was true whether I believed it or not. It was true whether I felt it or not. I couldn't wait until I had warm feelings about surrendering my life to Him. That might never happen! Freedom is the result of believing the truth (John 8:32), and believing the truth was something I could choose to do. To live according to my feelings would leave me a slave to those feelings.

On February 22nd, 2002, I chose to believe that what Scripture says about God is indeed true; to allow any contrary thoughts to enter my mind would mean defeat. My journal showed the evidence that

God was freeing me to worship Him. He gave me the grace to believe He is so good that if He were to take my life, He would be enough for my wife, enough for my kids, enough for our church, and enough for my parents and siblings.

Thank You for calling me Your "beloved." Thank You for the trial of cancer that has shown me that You are enough for joy. Your power and love are so great that not even cancer can remove that joy from my life. Thank You for communicating Your heart to me through Your Word. You are a wonderful, powerful Savior. To walk with You has been the greatest adventure of my life.

Lord, I open my hands to You. What You want is my desire. What You want is so much better than what I would seek to provide for myself. I want to receive from You. I choose to rest and stop trying to meet my own needs. You are my provider, my Master, my Lord and Savior, and I trust You. Have Your way in me.

CHAPTER 9

THE GOD WHO LEADS

Guiding people is an easy thing for the Almighty God. It seems that getting us to the place where we are willing to surrender to Him is the challenge in it all. As we continued to seek God for direction, He used a story about Jehoshaphat in 2 Chronicles 20 to speak to us. Jehoshaphat and the Israelites were facing a battle they didn't want to be part of. The army they were up against had far more soldiers and was far more powerful.

The first thing Jehoshaphat did was pray. He did not consult other people. He did not start barking orders to military officials. The only order he gave was for all the people of Judah to fast and pray, to seek the Lord. When he prayed, he prayed expectantly. He acknowledged the fact that the army coming against them was big, but in the same breath said, "No one can withstand You" (2 Chronicles 20:6).

I could have stood right alongside Jehoshaphat that day and agreed with everything he prayed. His battle was with Moabites. Mine, melanomacytes. Neither qualify as stressful or taxing to the infinite power of God. As I read this prayer again, I could almost hear the chains of fear falling away from the Israelites. The bigger God became in their eyes, the smaller their problem seemed, and the same was true of me.

As Jehoshaphat finished praying, he uttered a sentence that has been an oft-repeated prayer of my own. He said, "We have no power to attack this vast army that is attacking us. We do not know what to do, but our eyes are upon You." And then they stood before the Lord, hundreds of thousands of people . . . waiting.

THE BATTLE BELONGS TO THE LORD

It was as if God said to us, "That's what I want you to do! I want you to worship because I am huge, I am powerful, and I am so much bigger than cancer or a decision about where to get treated. When I fight, I never lose! Put your hope in Me. You can't do this on your own anyway. Just fix your eyes on Me!"

God's answer to Jehoshaphat and the rest of the Israelites was this: *"Do not be afraid or discouraged because of this vast army. For the battle is not yours but God's"* (2 Chronicles 20:15). It was becoming more and more clear to me that fear and discouragement are optional for the Christian. We don't have to live with these daggers of the enemy plunged into our backs!

After God had given them specific instructions about how they were to prepare for the battle, the people of Judah and Jerusalem began to worship. They took God at His Word, and they had the party *before* the victory even occurred! Now that is faith! The end result: God destroyed the opposing army without the men of Judah even having to pick up a weapon. God fought for them, and that is what He was promising to do for us. All we had to do was praise Him for being all that He is, and trust Him to show us what to do next. And show us He did!

Within a matter of days, God used a series of events and conversations to point us in one direction—Oasis of Hope Hospital in Tijuana, Mexico.

THE WEBSITE BEGINS

Shortly before we decided to go to Mexico, some friends suggested we start a website. Communicating with our families and friends had become a great challenge because there were so many people we cared about and wanted to keep updated. We just couldn't find the time. A website seemed like a great solution. I sent out an email telling our friends and families that they could check it any time for up-to-date prayer requests. On February 22nd, I put this note on the site:

Hi gang! Today has been an incredible day! Tammy and I snuck away to a camp up north in the woods so we could pray. We just wanted to be silent before the Lord to wait on Him before we make the next decision. It was awesome! God is clearly leading, and I'll tell you about that in a minute.

One thought that came to me today was this: I may have cancer in my body, and it is even possible that God will choose not to heal me. But, I do not have to be defeated by cancer, and I will not! It cannot make me depressed, it cannot steal my joy, it cannot cause me to be selfish, it cannot force me to worry. These are all choices I can make. Jesus died so I wouldn't have to be a slave to these things, and as long as I'm alive, I have a choice. I choose Christ!

OK, more good news—God seems to be paving the way for my next treatment. I can't go into all the details, but I can tell you I am convinced God wants me to receive treatment at the Oasis of Hope Hospital in Tijuana. It is an alternative medicine treatment center, and they have had remarkable results treating melanoma patients. They give non-toxic treatments intravenously, and will have me on a three-week program. The more I read about melanoma patients at this hospital, the more encouraged I become. The reason they are in Tijuana is primarily because the FDA will not allow them to use laetrile, one of their main cancer fighting agents, here in the US.

There is only one obstacle between us and this treatment center—the cashier's check for $22,750 that we have to provide up front. Gulp. Because it is an alternative medicine center, insurance won't cover it. It seems huge to us, but again, God has shown us hundreds of times that where He leads, He provides.

Please, do not feel pressured to participate in this financially. I'd rather have a root canal than for you to feel any kind of pressure. We are hoping to leave on Thursday or Friday of next week. I know it will take a miracle, but that is kind of what this whole thing has been about from the beginning.

Okay, that was one of my least favorite things to do in life—share a financial need— but several of you have asked how you can help, and maybe this is a way you can participate. For all its ups and downs, this sure has been an incredible ride. I can't wait to see what tomorrow brings! In case you've forgotten, we love you and are deeply grateful for your prayers!

Five days later, God completed the miracle of provision. I described it in my website journal entry:

Wednesday, February 27th, 2002

Yesterday I had the privilege of helping to wash the feet of a fellow minister as we prayed over him and sent him off to his next mission, which is a ministry in another city. The community leaders in Elk River meet every Tuesday to pray at noon, and we share some incredibly sweet fellowship—many denominations, one Lord. As we literally washed his feet, it struck me that Jesus Himself would have humbled Himself and honored this man by washing his feet. For some reason, I struggle to imagine the King of Kings and Lord of Lords washing my feet. I don't feel worthy.

But Jesus has washed our feet through you. You have prayed fervently for us, you have made meals for us, you have taken care of our kids, you have sent notes of encouragement, you have painted our bedrooms, you have blown snow out of our driveway when I was too weak to do it . . . the list goes on and on. And now you have paid the entire hospital bill at Oasis of Hope. We reached our goal tonight in just days. $23,000. What in the world can I say but, "Thank you, Lord!" I feel like I have just opened a gift, and God has been watching, waiting, and smiling with anticipation as He watches the look on our faces. Could it be that He delights to provide for us, to bless us, to meet our every need?

We are humbled and incredibly blessed by your sacrificial love. I feel like I have just witnessed a miracle. Why in the world do I ever doubt Him? I think I'm going to have a hard time going to sleep tonight.

We love you . . . and thank you again for making the love of God real and present to us.

Dan

CHAPTER 10

THE DEEP, DEEP LOVE OF JESUS

The more that God set us free from the need to be in control of our lives, the more we begin to understand just how much He loves us. My web journal entry on February 28th was an expression of what was happening in our hearts as we prepared to leave for Mexico:

It is hard for me to know where to begin as I seek to describe what this week has been like. I have simply been overwhelmed by the love of God. There have been a multitude of things I thought would satisfy me over the course of my life, but they have all been cheap substitutes for intimacy with the Lord Jesus. I am sensing the satisfaction of being totally and passionately loved by God.

This love doesn't fail or let me down. It never goes away. It is vast, unmeasured, boundless, and free. It is undeserved. It flows from the heart of God, tumbling out, falling down upon me. It covers me—as my friend wrote today—like a warm, soft, fresh-out-of-the-dryer blanket. It won't let me go. It fills me up, leaves me lacking for nothing.

I don't know how long I'll live, but in reality, neither do you. I'll plead with you—if you've never put your hope in God, don't wait another day! Life is too short to waste it on cheap thrills, nice stuff, and meaningless accomplishments. I can honestly say that I have never had so much joy as I have had since being diagnosed with cancer. All that is meaningless has been stripped away. Loving God and loving people have become paramount. Life has never been so good.

THIS PLACE IS INCREDIBLE

We were filled with anticipation and a little apprehension as we boarded the airplane for San Diego. My mind raced as I contemplated what it would be like to receive health care in a foreign country. *What will God do in Mexico? What will He show*

92

us? Will the treatment work? What if the American doctor was right when he said, 'If there was anything that good down there we would have it here.'

God put many of my fears to rest within the first hour of our arrival at the hospital. As we walked in the door, we were greeted by a large, framed Bible verse on the wall. It was Isaiah 41:13, which reads, "For I am the Lord, your God, who takes hold of your right hand and says to you, Do not fear; I will help you." The theme of God's help in the midst of fearful situations had been written on our lives in the previous months. It was God's way of saying to me, "You are right where I want you."

Shortly after arriving, we were ushered into an office where we would meet the doctor handling my case. Dr. Gutierrez introduced himself and gave me a physical examination. When he finished, he said some things I will never forget.

"Mr. and Mrs. Roelofs, I want to explain a little bit about how we operate at Oasis of Hope. First, there are things that we will do for you." One by one, Dr. Gutierrez explained how the staff at Oasis would administer my treatment. "Then there are things we expect you to do." Staying with the pre- scribed diet, going to classes held in the hospital, exercising, and other similar things were on this next list. Then he got a very focused look on his face and said, "The last category is a list of things that neither you nor the staff at Oasis can do. These are the things we must trust God to do, and that is why we pray." With that, he grabbed Tammy's hand and my own hand and prayed the most passionate prayer I have ever heard a doctor pray. Actually, it's the only prayer I've heard a doctor pray in my presence. It was beautiful.

As Tammy and I walked out of his office and down the hall toward our room, I looked at her and gushed, "This place is incredible!" We prayed a prayer of gratitude that night for all that God had done in leading us to this place where we sensed His love and power so mightily.

Over the next three weeks, I felt like I had been personally invited by God to come away from life as I knew it to simply be in His presence. He had so much to share, so many good gifts to give. It was like an intimate conversation with a best friend at a table for two in a really nice restaurant.

I had taken a book with me, written by John Eldredge and Brent Curtis, called *The Sacred Romance*. One paragraph from that book described what God was doing in my heart. The authors' perspective was that Satan seeks to "replace the love affair with a religious system of do's and don'ts that parches our hearts and replaces our worship and communion services with entertainment. Our experience of life deteriorates from the passion of a love affair, in the midst of a life and death battle to an endless series of chores and errands, a busyness that separates us from God, each other, and even from our own thirstiness." This had been true of me, and now God was calling me away from this to let my heart engage with the One who made me.

An excerpt from my March 7th web journal entry describes this process in more detail:

> *The time hooked up to machines has been a great blessing. It has forced me to sit and do nothing for a period of time, and I have come to appreciate this. It has caused me to slow down, to "be still and know that He is God," as Psalm 46:10 says. The last few months I have felt very pursued by God. I'm a little embarrassed that it took cancer to really get my attention, but it is an incredible thing to think about the fact that God will go to great lengths to show us how much He loves us. I feel like Tammy and I have been sent to Tijuana so we will stop and listen to God while He explains how deeply He is in love with us.*

It is hard to deny His existence as I sit on the beach watching ocean waves crashing against the shore as the sun comes up in the morning. I have done a lot of talking to God in my life, but I haven't done a bunch of listening. I am learning the joy of listening, but still wrestle with the thought that the King would actually want to communicate with me. However, I know it's true, and if this were all I had to cling to it would be enough. And if it's true of me, it's true of you, too. Today. Even now. It's clear to me now that I don't have anything more important to do than to listen.

On March 9th, I again tried to explain what God was teaching me about His love in my website journal:

I was awake late last night, reading the lyrics to several hymns in a hymnal I was given to prepare for the Sunday service. There is one that brings tears to my eyes every time we sing it at Woodland, and even as I read the words now: "O, The Deep, Deep Love of Jesus." Here are a few lyrics:

"O, the deep, deep love of Jesus, vast unmeasured, boundless, free.

Rolling as a mighty ocean in its fullness

over me.

Underneath me all around me, is the current of Thy love.

Leading onward, leading homeward, to Thy glorious rest above."

Another verse says,

"'Tis an ocean vast of blessing, 'tis a haven sweet of rest.

O the deep, deep love of Jesus, 'tis a heaven of heavens to me.

And it lifts me up to glory for it lifts me up to Thee."

The words of this song echo in my mind as I walk along the ocean. It is high tide right now, and the waves are crashing hard. I've been overwhelmed by waves before, and right now I feel overwhelmed by the love of God. Maybe I sound like a broken record. It's just that I can't imagine ever being satisfied with anything else again. The world has nothing to equal it.

There is no success, no measure of the approval of people, no material possession, or even an earthly relationship that could ever compare to the deep, deep love of Jesus. The more I get lost in it, the more I forget I'm even sick. If I didn't have tubes coming from my chest, I wouldn't remember. What in the world is there to fear in the face of this kind of love? What is there to worry about? What is there to be irritated by? What is there to be bitter about?

We tend to define ourselves by what people say about us, or by what we do—whether that be good or bad. I'm a teacher, I'm a farmer, I'm a businessman, or even spiritually—I'm a failure, I'm a regular church-goer, or I'm addicted to this or that. The truth is, I am one who is constantly being pursued by the deep, deep love of Jesus. And the miracle about this pursuit is that He is not trying to catch up with me to give me what I deserve. He pursues me in order to bless. I am His child. Unbelievable. How can I do anything but surrender and worship?

CHAPTER 11

SURRENDER

The treatment program at Oasis of Hope was 21 days. The doctors ordered a CT scan right away when I arrived, and then planned another one for the day before we left. The intent was to determine the effectiveness of the treatment while we were still there. As the second scan approached, it became evident to me that trust and surrender would need to be a daily decision. There seemed to be so much riding on this one scan. I knew that we were never beyond the reach of God, and I planned to keep fighting until Jesus took me home, but Oasis felt like our last chance.

God reminded me once again that His desire for me was rest and surrender. As I listened to Him about what this meant, I wrote this journal entry on the website the day before the scan:

Surrender. It's a word that has been easy to sing about or read about in someone else's life, but vastly different to live out. It essentially means to give up the control you once had to another. To quit resisting. To give up your own agenda. I have thought about it more the last couple days because this week I will have "the scan." It's a moment I have thought about and prayed about for quite some time already.

Back in November, three weeks before being diagnosed, I sensed a change coming from God. I wrote in my devotional journal, "I sense that God wants me to open myself up to Him to experience Him in ways that I never have before, and that I shouldn't be fearful about what's ahead." The entry was the result of reading Jeremiah 10:23, which says, "I know, O Lord, that a man's life is not his own; it is not for man to direct his steps."

The prayer that followed in my journal said, "Direct my life, Lord. Make my steps useful for Your kingdom, for the glory of Your name. I release my life to You today. I trust You to lead me. I abandon myself to Your love."

Back then it was true in principle. Now I can

choose to make it true in reality. It is time to live out what it means to abandon myself to His love. When you have laid down everything about your life before God, fear cannot remain—there is nothing more that can be taken away. I have the one thing I desire, and that is Christ.

John 12:24 and 25 were verses that shaped my vision for our new church. I knew if God were to really bless us, and grant us influence, it would be the result of living out these verses. "I tell you the truth, unless a kernel of wheat falls to the ground and dies, it remains only a single seed. But if it dies, it produces many seeds. The man who loves his life will lose it, while the man who hates his life in this world will keep it for eternal life."

One by one, God has been stripping away all the things that I hold on to, things that are not Him. There was a time when I feared this. But now I am seeing that whenever He takes something away, it is only to give me something better in return. His life for mine, His joy exchanged for worldly pleasure. There is something more valuable to be gained here than health, and it is Christ.

Please pray that God will protect us from

fear as the scan approaches—I think it will be happening on Thursday. Pray that our emotions would not be tied to anything but the truth about who God is. Pray that we will continue to worship, regardless of the outcome. If God gives us the ability to do this, cancer will never defeat us!

Thanks.

Dan

Two days later the scan results came back, and here is the report I left on the website.

Friday, March 22nd, 2002

Praise God! The tumors haven't grown! The doctor just came with the scan results, and the size of the tumors is the same as when we checked in. This is the first scan that hasn't shown growth since this whole adventure began.

I woke up scared this morning. I couldn't get the scan off my mind. The words of Psalm 91 came to mind again, and I just began praying them back to the Lord. The fear disappeared immediately. I just realized that trusting God and giving Him glory in this situation are impossible for me. And that is why I need Him. It is His strength, His joy, His love, His protection,

His very life—that have sustained my family and me for the past four months. Praise God that His resources never run out, and they are never more than a simple prayer away. Every time I have called on Him, He has answered. Every single time.

Your prayers are so precious to me. Please don't stop. I have a sense that this battle is just beginning, and even though I truly believe God intends for me to survive, I know the healing is a process. It is in the waiting that we are changed. It's not what I would prefer, but I'm not in charge (and that's a good thing!).

For today, I'm not going to focus on the weeks and months ahead. I'm just thanking God for the good news! I think we'll go to Sea World to celebrate!

Three months later found us returning to the hospital for another scan. It seemed like an eternity since I had last taken a look inside my body via technology to see what the cancer was doing. I will never forget the day the doctor called me with the results.

Results are in . . . I'm screaming, but you probably can't hear me! The tumors are shrink-

ing!! All the tumors on my right lung . . . gone! The large tumor on my left lung has shrunk in half since the last scan. There is no other detectable cancer in my body!!! The lymph nodes in my groin have been swollen and palpable for the last few months, and I feared that this was cancer, too, but haven't been talking about it. Now I finally know that it is just backed up lymph, not cancer.

Tammy just looked at me after I got off the phone with the doctor and said, "You're going to get to watch your kids grow up!" Then we cried and hugged. I'm struggling to grasp all that is going on right now. I can't even describe the emotion. Everything about "incurable disease" that I've heard in the last several months is out the window! I know that I am not yet healed completely, but the fact that the cancer is going the opposite direction is nothing short of a miracle. Thank God for another day of life!!!

Thank you for praying and giving and serving and loving us. You have all helped to make this day a reality. I know we still have a long road ahead of us, but this gives incredible motivation to keep fighting. Thank you.

Lord God, more than anyone else I want to

thank You. You have been my rock. You have been the friend who is closer than a brother. You have been everything I have needed at every moment in this journey. You are my reason for living, and I love You more than words could ever express. Thank You for all these incredible people You have brought around us to help me fight. Nothing is too difficult for You, and I can't praise You enough. Bless everyone who reads this in the same way that they have blessed my family and me. Thanks for every breath. I know each one is a gift.

Your kid,

Dan

WHERE HAS THE PASSION GONE?

As I write, there is a bullfight going on across the street from my hospital room in Tijuana. It strikes me as crazy that someone would put their life in danger to entertain a crowd as they dance with *el toro*. In the end, it is a pretty meaningless battle. However, it's a battle the matador chooses to fight.

It reminds me of a much more significant battle happening in the heavenly realm. Every one of us is a part of it, whether we choose to be or not. Satan, our spiritual enemy, is doing all he can to lure our hearts away from the One who alone can satisfy them. He has a well-developed arsenal of weapons and uses them quite effectively to steal the hearts of men and women. Oh, it's not always through drugs, sex, and rock and roll. He doesn't need them. We're too busy. We're already right where he wants us— knowing lots of things about God, but never really knowing God.

We have other pursuits, of course, that are very important. God is important, too, for sure. But what exactly would God ask of us? We already go to church regularly, serve on a committee, and pray before meals. My goodness, we might even help our children memorize Bible verses for Sunday school.

And so we fill our lives with the things our hearts are really passionate about—our careers, our hobbies, our friends, our toys. And God looks on with love in His eyes and says, "If you'll hold on to Me for dear life, I'll get you out of any trouble. I'll give you the best of care if you'll only get to know and trust Me. Call Me and I'll answer, be at your side in bad times; I'll rescue you, then throw you a party." (Psalm 91, *The Message Bible*).

Satan's goal has been accomplished when we trade the one thing our soul longs for more than anything else, for stuff. For good jobs, nice cars, comfortable houses, and a better golf game. And our hearts become dulled. Passionless. Even. . . dead.

I know. I've been there.

But the Great Pursuer of Our Hearts continues His relentless quest to bless—to give life to passionless hearts—to give meaning to lives without purpose. He yearns to give freedom to those who are chained to things they don't want to be doing or feeling or even remembering. He longs to grant us a new identity, a new label for our lives: Pursued by God, Child of God, God's Beloved, Friend of God, Servant of God.

In pain and in pleasure, in things that are outwardly beautiful and in things that are not, in successes and failures, God is speaking, and He's speaking to our hearts. Scripture makes it clear that it is our hearts—the center of our affections—that God is after: "Trust in the Lord with all your heart" (Proverbs 3:5); "Seek me with all your heart" (Jeremiah 29:13); "Love the Lord your God with all your heart" (Deuteronomy 30:10); "Where your treasure is, there will your heart be also" (Matthew 6:21); ". . . doing the will of God from your heart" (Ephesians 6:6). The list of Scriptures referring to God's pursuit of our hearts goes on and on. God is about a relationship, and there is no relationship without a passionately involved heart.

WHAT WE ASKED FOR

I am amazed at how difficult it is to stop checking email, turn off phones, and put away the to-do list. However, as difficult as it may be, my soul desperately needs it. I'm finding that there is no amount of sleep, no amount of NFL football, no amount of being entertained that really refreshes me the way I am refreshed when God breaks the silence and lets me hear His voice. To encounter Him is to encounter passion, energy, and refreshment.

I need to be reminded that no matter how fast I may run, I won't be satisfied unless it is Him I'm pursuing. One thing this cancer journey has revealed is how many other things I've been chasing—worthless things, really, especially when compared to the thrill of being in the presence of the One who spoke the universe into existence. And to think He knows my name. Unbelievable.

Tammy hid Reid's blanket the other day. Wow, did he cry. But it only lasted a couple minutes, and he hasn't missed it since. (He had previously been attached to it like a slug on a rock.) I feel like God is doing that in my life—using great pressure to pry away things I didn't need but really wanted. And to be honest, sometimes I feel like Reid bawling on the floor. I asked God today why it hurts so much. He seemed to say that sometimes idols have to be smashed to pieces before we stop trying to suck life out of them—before we stop trying to make them fill us up. I know He does it to give me something far greater—the gift of Himself.

When I worked with Freedom in Christ, my friend Dave Park and I spent numerous nights away from home doing conferences for youth. On many occasions, we stayed up late into the night talking and praying. A recurring theme of those prayers was an expressed hunger and deep desire to know and experience God. To hear Him, to touch Him, to taste of Him, to see Him—it's really all we wanted.

In talking with Dave the other day, my perspective was once again altered as we discussed the role of pain in our lives. "We shouldn't be surprised at these challenges. God is simply answering our prayer. This is what we asked for," Dave said to me. Indeed it is.

CHAPTER 12

BACK IN THE BATTLE

My battle with cancer was not yet finished. In early November, 2002 we received new scan results. They were not what we were hoping for. Both of the tumors on my left lung had grown since the September scan and both had increased in size by about 30 percent. Tammy called me with the news, since I was in South Carolina visiting my friend Ross and his family. There, I had enjoyed the privilege of sharing my testimony at North Hills Community Church. So many people there had prayed for me, and I had longed to meet them. It was great to worship with them and see their faces.

After talking to Tammy and my other family members on the phone, Ross and I drove to a lake situated in the hills, with the Blue Ridge Mountains in the distance. We sat in silence while we watched God do His thing—birds singing, leaves changing colors, the glorious sun setting. It had been cloudy all day, but during the last half hour before the sun went down, the clouds parted and the sun spread its brilliance across the sky. We prayed and once again entrusted our lives into God's hands. It gave me great comfort to know that my life is in the hands of the God who spoke the lake, the birds, the mountains, and the sunset into existence.

I soon found myself again in 2 Chronicles 20—the same passage God gave me the day after we were told by doctors in Illinois that there was nothing more they could do. It was here God said, "You will not have to fight this battle. It is the Lord's." The people of Judah chose to worship God, and God fought for them. They didn't have to strategize or figure out how to solve the problem. That wasn't what God wanted from them. He wanted their worship, their adoration, and their undivided attention. They worshiped, and God destroyed their enemy. What a plan! God's word to Judah was His word to me. *You worship, I'll fight.* That truth continued to free me to trust Him.

A DIFFICULT DECISION

The new cancer growth prompted an evaluation of what I needed to change in fighting this disease. After seeking the Lord and talking with my doctor, my mentor, and several friends, I made one of the most difficult decisions I've ever had to make in my life. I told Woodland Fellowship I was stepping down from my role as pastor. Leading a church while battling cancer had never been easy, but at the same time I had always known it wasn't about taking the easy road. It was about obedience to God. I knew He had called me to plant that church, and therefore stepping down was never an option in my mind—until November 2002. Several things happened in rapid succession that led me to believe the best thing for my health and the well-being of my family was for me to step down.

I'm not sure which was more difficult—making the decision or telling the people I love. Fortunately, God gave me the strength I needed to communicate with the people of our church the reasons that led me to believe this is what He wanted for me.

Unsure of what would come next, I was sure we could continue to trust God. On November 25th, the day after my resignation message, I posted the following thoughts in my journal:

We've taken another step in the journey. God's presence is as real now as it ever has been, and for that we are grateful. It has been difficult, but we are not discouraged. God has been so faithful to speak to us and reveal His will to us. Regardless of where I am or what I'm doing, I will continue to write and speak about the God I'm in love with. He has always provided for us before, and I have no reason to start doubting Him now. There is unbelievable comfort in knowing He has ordered this step, and He's walking with us. In one sense, it feels like the weight of the world (this decision) has been removed from my shoulders!

JOY CONTINUES

Within a very short time, God was sending us all kinds of encouragement. First of all, Freedom in Christ Ministries invited me to join the staff as one of their communicators. The aim of the ministry is to use conferences, books, and videos as an avenue to share life-changing truth with teens, college students, and adults. Tammy and I had previously worked with FIC as interns from 1994-1996. It was a great experience for us, and the staff members there were still dear friends.

The ministry was based in Knoxville, Tennessee, but it was not necessary for us to move there. The intention of this step was for me to focus as much energy as possible on fighting cancer, but to still have an outlet to share the wonders of the grace of God in our lives through speaking and writing.

Another unexpected encouragement came from the leadership of the Baptist General Conference, the denomination in which I had pastored. They called and said, "We were talking about how we might be a support to you and your family during this time. How would you like to go to Cozumel in the next two weeks?" Cozumel is a resort island in Mexico, and these men had access to a condo that wasn't being rented in December. So, they sent our whole family to the beach on this tropical island for a week! It was an unbelievable gift—a family memory to be cherished forever.

We spent time at the beach every day—snorkeling, swimming, and relaxing. It was just what the doctor ordered. It was the first time I had snorkeled in the ocean, and the first time I had been in water for a year. The nurses removed my port needle so I wouldn't risk an infection and told me to have at it! It was awesome! The colors were incredible, and I had no idea there were so many different kinds of fish.

We were also able to step back from our busy lives in order to listen more attentively to God and to enjoy each other. We just had a good, old fashioned blast!

The year that had seemed so uncertain on the front end drew to a close with me saying:

I have officially wrapped up my responsibilities as pastor and I can see that God is removing yet another prop in our lives to keep us totally dependent on Him. Where once this situation would have created great fear, it is now giving us a sense of joy and anticipation. Whenever God has taken away something that we were depending on apart from Him, His replacement has been incredible. We have come to expect that. I can honestly say there is no way I'd rather live.

What a joy it is to celebrate Christmas with my family. A year ago I only hoped I'd see this day. I am so grateful!

CHAPTER 13

CLINGING TO GOD

Early in January, I began to feel a lump on my back—just to the left of my spine. The doctor said it was definitely not muscle or normal growth, so I had an extensive CT scan of my chest and abdomen. The day of the scan, I battled fear off and on all day as I awaited the results, and the clinic never called. I had trouble falling asleep that evening, and as I poured out my heart to God, His peace once again filled me. He faithfully met me and gave me a new perspective on the whole situation. As it had been each step of this road, the outward, physical stuff was just a tool in God's hand.

He was definitely teaching me again. Everything was laid bare, and I was clinging to God with everything in me. I was also praising Him. To know joy

and peace in the midst of a trial like this was nothing less than supernatural. I had deep confidence
that neither life, nor death, nor angels, nor demons,
nor anything else in all creation, could separate me
from the love of God that is in Christ!

THE DREADED NEWS

The scan results came the next day and two days
later, I shared the news with the many faithful
prayer warriors who were following my situation
on the website:

Saturday, January 11th, 2003

*The scan results were less than favorable.
The word "multiple" was used several times in
the report, each time referring to new tumor
growth—kidneys, adrenal glands, and un-
attached in my abdomen. Lung tumors still
growing.*

*As you can imagine, the news threw us for a
loop. I put my head down on my desk and wanted to cry, but tears wouldn't come. I went for a
walk, because Tammy wasn't home yet to share
the news with. When I came back, she had seen
the fax on my desk and was trembling.*

*We have since done much talking and pray-
ing together. Last night we left town and went to*

a bed and breakfast to pray. God gave Tammy a wonderful night of sleep (she hadn't slept much the night before), and He met us in the Word again. Just hearing His voice makes any challenge seem not-so-insurmountable. I went back to the passages that have meant so much to us— Psalm 91, 2 Chronicles 20, and Psalm 116.

We are assured of His love, and know that our only rest is in surrender. God is asking us to lay down everything that we would cling to in order for us to fully embrace Him, even if that means my life. In the end, we will know Him more intimately, trust Him absolutely, and obey Him more faithfully. He is teaching us so much! His love truly is better than life! I feel like I am beginning to understand what it means to hold nothing back from God and to free-fall into His strong arms. I feel so safe in Him.

We sense God leading us back to Oasis of Hope Hospital in Mexico. We are hoping that what worked the first time to turn the tide will work again. We are planning to leave in about a week if God grants us the funds to go. Why do I say if? I know that He will if that is where He wants us.

GOD SHOWED UP!

Just two days later, I was in Iowa to spend time with my mom and dad while speaking at Western Christian High School. These postings from the website tell the story:

Monday—*Thank you for praying for me this morning. God gave me the strength to give a message to the students at Western Christian, and I sensed the presence and power of God in the chapel service. Pray for those who gave their hearts to Christ this morning.*

Tuesday—*Those of you who are praying for our time at Western Christian High School need to know that prayers are being answered! God is breaking down walls and students are opening up to us about their lives. There has been a distinct sense of the Holy Spirit's presence during chapel. One more day tomorrow—can't wait to see what God does!*

Wednesday—*I have been involved in ministry for several years, yet I've never seen a move of God like I observed this week at Western Christian High School. I now have a little better understanding of why there was so much spiritual warfare last week. God had plans that none of us knew about, and it was beautiful to watch.*

It is hard to put into words what happened in the

chapel services. It was as if God came and pitched His tent and just poured out His love on the students there. They responded with passion. When the final chapel was over, the worship team invited the audience to applaud the God who had visited us. They gave God a standing ovation that seemed to go on and on. It brings tears to my eyes every time I think about it.

After the last chapel was complete, about 20-25 students gathered around to pray for me, pouring out their hearts to God on my behalf. I couldn't contain my emotion—not only because I was touched by their love, but because my heart was so full of gratitude to God for what He had done in these students' lives. On their own, the students at the school initiated a medical expense fund for me and collected over $10,000. Can you believe that?!

I also got to visit Hull Christian School and Rock Valley Christian School. Both groups of students and staff have prayed fervently for us and have been incredibly gracious to us. I drove back to Minneapolis feeling unbelievably blessed by God for His grace to me this week, and ready to pack my bags for another trip to the cancer hospital in Tijuana.

CHAPTER 14

FEAR AND FREEDOM

January 23rd, 2003

Now would be a good time to say, "Hola, amigos!" We made it safely to San Diego ahead of all the Super Bowlers and were picked up by the hospital shuttle van to be brought to Oasis. Our prayer while we are here is that we can continue to focus on what God is teaching us, and what He's saying to us, instead of on the medical situation.

We walked on the boardwalk this morning for a half hour and that did me in for the rest of the morning. I did my other treatments but was exhausted, and spent most of the morning in bed. I don't have the stamina I used to have, and it's hard for me to accept that. The battle we fight is an effort to keep our eyes on the Lord and His goodness when everything natural about us wants to focus on the physical issues. More symptoms are popping up, and they beg for my attention.

There was a time when this battle was purely spiritual and emotional. It is now becoming physical, as well. This simply means we need to be prepared to fight every minute of the day. The symptoms can either discourage and distract, or they can be a reminder of our absolute dependence on God. For today, I choose to depend and rest! God continually reminds me that even though the opposing army is getting bigger in my eyes, it is no more difficult for Him to heal now than it was when the tumors were smaller.

God reminded me in my devotions about all the ways He has met us since this journey began. I was amazed as I once again thought about His faithfulness to us, and the love He has shown us. He has been so personal, so real, so obviously passionate in His love toward us. Looking back with a grateful heart makes looking ahead so much easier.

January 25th, 2003

Buck and his wife Phyllis are two rooms down from us. Buck just burst into our room with tears in his eyes. I thought he wanted us to pray for him or something. Instead, he had come to tell us that the tumor on Phyllis's liver had shrunk by 40% while they have been here. He was so overwhelmed with joy he hugged us both. We just met him two days ago, but relationships go deep pretty quickly here!

Tammy went in to talk to Phyllis after she heard the news, and Phyllis told her she'd read my book while she and Buck were waiting for her scan results. She told Tammy that for the first time ever, she'd made a conscious decision to surrender her life to Christ as she finished the book. What a gift from the Lord the book has been—to us first and foremost!

Tammy said to me last night, "The message of this book is really for us, isn't it?"

"Yep," I responded. We are the ones He has desired to lead to a place called Surrender. We are the ones who need to see His face in the midst of the pain. We are the ones who have been blessed with a joy that has nothing to do with circumstances.

The message of the book is that this present trial is another opportunity, an opportunity to encounter Him—the Source of Joy. It's an opportunity to experience His sufficiency in ways we have never known before because the pit is deeper now, the water is higher, and the enemies are more numerous. In the midst of all this, the rest is sweeter. The victory is greater. His presence is more discernible.

"He reached down from on high and took hold of me; He drew me out of deep waters. He rescued me from my powerful enemy, from my foes, who were too strong for me. They confronted me in the day of my disaster, but the Lord was my support. He brought me out into a spacious place; He rescued me because He delighted in me." (Psalm 18:16-19)

BECOMING GOD'S FRIEND
January 29th, 2003

After a week of waiting on the Lord, I feel like He is finally communicating with me. I know it is probably more a matter of me being ready to listen, so I'm not complaining! I haven't shared much about what's happening with us spiritually and emotionally, so I'll attempt to do that today. I'm not into facades, so here we go . . .

This past week has been one of the most spiritually intense and difficult since this journey began. In the past, whenever I have had burdens, I took them to Jesus and they disappeared. Peace and joy and encouragement have always been the result. His presence has sustained us for the past 14 months. Living in a place called Surrender was the joy of our lives.

This past week has been different. I have still been taking the burdens to Him, but my heart has been heavy nonetheless. I don't know why, except that I feel like God is allowing me to grieve what I have lost, and what I may be losing. I'm not healthy anymore. I hurt in places I didn't used to hurt, and I cannot do some things I once did. These physical issues put the loss right back in front of my face, tempting me to despair, to give up. Especially when I think about the fact that if the disease progresses, pain will increase, and the treatment I have coming soon is supposed to make me very sick.

In addition, the patients at Oasis this time are for the most part very ill. The last time we were here, there were more people who had cancer but were symptom-free, just as I was.

Not this trip. One gal who attended Prayer & Share with us a week ago passed away last night. Others are really struggling. Mealtimes were once full of laughter and encouragement, and lately have seemed more discouraging as people discuss the incredible pain in their lives. The pictures we have posted online may be a little misleading about what life in the hospital is really like.

The previous thoughts are all from a very human point of view. Very real, but very slanted from a human perspective. Today God changed all that.

I've been studying the life of Abraham lately. I can relate to him on so many different fronts. This study asked some questions that nailed the issue going on in my heart. The first question: Are you willing to leave your family and your country to follow God? My interpretation: Are you willing to go where God wants you to go, even if it means great pain or suffering for yourself? Next question: Are you willing for God to do anything to shape and mold your life? If you are, explain how you know that. If not, what is keeping you from that kind of relationship with God?

It was like God was saying to Abraham, "Any country, any place won't do! It is the place I choose where I will shape you and make you My friend." I am learning that love involves a release of one's life unconditionally to God. Unconditionally. What a word! To unconditionally say "yes" to God is to stand before Him in absolute nakedness, in absolute trust, willing to walk in absolute obedience. That is surrender! Do you honestly know anyone who lives that way? That kind of trust and obedience would turn the world upside down for the glory of God!

God was committed to refining and shaping Abraham because He wanted the absolute best for him. The same is true for me. Every challenge I face is carefully crafted by God to help me reach my maximum potential. Abraham did not have to shape himself. He didn't have to develop his faith. All he had to do was respond in trust and obedience, a step at a time.

My answer to the questions: I am willing. There are times when I fear the pain that I know He may choose to use to shape me, but I know He is an expert refiner. He knows just how hot to make the fire. I know, too, that He refines me because He loves me and is making me His friend. And that is what I want more than healing, more than freedom from pain, more than anything.

It is nothing less than the grace of God that has freed my heart today. He is doing the same in Tammy. I can see it in her eyes. I believe this grace has come to us because of your prayers. I unashamedly ask that you would continue.

PERFECT TIMING
February 7th, 2003

Today was a day in the fire. More new tumors appeared. My cough keeps getting worse. I have no energy. I just want to sleep. Yes, today was a day in the fire. But God was in the fire with us. Like the Apostle Paul said, "We are hard pressed on every side, but not crushed; perplexed, but not in despair; persecuted, but not abandoned; struck down, but not destroyed. We always carry around in our body the death of Jesus so that the Life of Jesus may also be revealed in our body" (2 Corinthians 4:8-10). Thank you so much for praying these realities into our lives.

I continue to be overwhelmed by the num-

ber of people who have taken the time to communicate with us. I cry when I get mail. It is just very emotional to know that God is telling me He loves us through all of you. I couldn't sense His presence last night at 3:00 a.m. when I felt lousy, but I am reminded of all the ways He has demonstrated His love, and I can't help but be encouraged. Tammy brought up the mail today, and we must've had at least 20 pieces. It was so awesome! I sat and read notes from people all over the country. The mail truck didn't come the last couple of days but now I know why—God was storing it up for me, knowing that today was the day I would need to read it.

I'll share two poems from elementary students (which blew me away) and a comforting verse that came in the mail:

Long, long ago in a far away land,
God made a special man, his name was Dan.
He was tall, he was not small!
Big in my heart he will always be
He was the one who taught faith to me.
(by Alexandra MacDonald, age 8)

"This is what the Lord says—he who created you . . . 'Fear not, for I have redeemed you; I have summoned you by name; you are mine. When you pass through the waters, I will be with you; when you pass through the rivers, they will not sweep over you. When you walk through the fire, you will not be burned; the flames will not set you ablaze. For I am the Lord, your God, the Holy One of Israel, your Savior." (Isaiah 43:1-3 - Thanks, Katie!)

Always cares
Brave and strong describe him well
Always looks away from himself
Looks like inspiration to me.
Has cancer
Never gives up when the going gets rough
Still wants to serve God
Sounds like perseverance to me.
Paving the way so I can see
The way that God has called for me
Looks like significance to me.
Dan
The person I admire
My example
My good friend
(by Claire Robinson, age 11)

132

CHAPTER 15

THE GREATEST GIFT

I just can't imagine how people go through something like cancer without God. His Word has been my lifeline. He has blanketed me with His peace. He has been with me through this whole ordeal—right from the first day. In fact, He has been with me for a lot longer than that and I know I can never take that for granted. A personal relationship with the one true God is the most valuable thing any person can have.

I am so glad I heard the truth about who He is and how desperately I needed Him back when I was fourteen. To be honest, when I called out to Jesus for salvation and made that decision to follow Him, I had no idea the difference it would make in my life. But today, I am sure I could never have made it without Him. And I certainly don't want anyone else trying to make it without Him, either. There is no reason for that. God has already done the work. All we have to do is come to the end of ourselves and believe Him.

THE REAL DISEASE
February 3rd, 2003

Terminal. That's the word used by traditional doctors for people like me with melanoma. I don't have a Webster's handy to look it up, but I'm assuming if I did, I would find descriptions like: dead end, the end, with no more continuation, without an outlet. As I talk with other cancer patients, I realize almost all of us have been told that we are without hope.

Maybe that's how you feel about your life. It is possible you don't need a doctor to tell you things are not going as they should be, and maybe you are starting to lose hope. The Bible offers a perspective about why that might be the case.

We were all born into the world with a disease; the disease is called sin. Some people don't even know they have it, but it has disastrous effects, regardless. Sin isn't simply the tendency to do bad things. At its root, sin is simply that innate part of us that does not want to submit to God. We would rather have our own way. We want to be independent—calling our own shots.

The effect of all this is separation from God. Alienation. Distance. Lack of relationship. Lack of intimacy. There are many who would claim to believe in God, but they are simply referring to an intellectual assent to the idea that there is a God. Unfortunately, this does not end the alienation. Believing there is a God does not end loneliness, or put a marriage back together, or end depression, or give joy to a downcast heart. It doesn't give meaning to life or satisfaction in one's deepest parts. It doesn't bring forgiveness of sin.

Scripture tells us this disease of sin is terminal. Romans 6:23 states, "The wages of sin is death"—not only physical death, but spiritual death. Separation from God for all eternity. That is the ultimate definition of terminal. A death sentence for sure.

But God did not create us to be alienated from Him. He did not intend us to live with this sin disease and have no hope. He is the Great Physician, and He is also a passionate Lover. It grieves Him deeply to be separated from the children He created—those He loves so deeply. His heartfelt desire is that none would be terminal, but that all would come to repentance. But what about the disease?

God dealt our sin disease a fatal blow when He sent His Son, Jesus Christ, to be born into this world, right alongside us, to live a perfect life and then to die on a cross. His death was the sacrifice that paid the penalty of sin for you and me. He became our substitute. His shed blood was like the vaccine that could cleanse us of our disease and restore us to intimacy with God. Powerful!

Because of this sacrifice, those who were once terminal can now have the hope of life, and life eternal! Jesus said, "I have come that they may have life, and that they may have it more abundantly" (John 10:10). This life is found in a relationship with the Great Physician, the Creator of the World, the Author of Life, the Lover of our Souls. Do you have that kind of life? Do you want it? Your life doesn't have to be one dead end after another. God has pleasures waiting for you in Him that makes the temporary happiness of this world look like Monopoly money. Life in Christ is the real thing!

AGREEING WITH GOD

You can be reconciled to God right now! Scripture says we need to first agree with God that we are sinful. Then we need to recognize that there is no other solution for that sin disease than putting our faith in Jesus Christ. This is why Jesus Christ is called a Savior. He is the source of the only vaccine that will help us. Going to church doesn't erase sin. Being a good person doesn't cure it. Only the blood of Jesus Christ can make us whole again. When you believe that, you can cry out to God and by faith say, "God, I'm putting my hope in You!" The Bible says, "Believe in the Lord Jesus Christ and you will be saved"(Acts 16:31).

If you're not sure what to say to God, here are some words to guide you: "Heavenly Father, Awesome God, I want to know You! I want to experience Your love and every good plan that You have for my life. I've done life on my own for quite awhile. I know I've resisted You without even knowing it at times. I want that to end today. I submit my life to You. Forgive my sin, Lord. Cleanse me of all the things I've done that have hurt You. I believe You are the Way to eternal life. I put my trust in You. I want to follow You all the days of my life and be in Your presence for all eternity. I receive You as my Lord and Savior. Thank You for making me Your child. I love You."

If you prayed that prayer, you are no longer terminal. Praise God, neither am I! I never will be! No matter what.

CHAPTER 16

OPEN DOORS

[Note to the reader: Dan reached a point physically where he could not write often. The rest of his story, however, is recorded here for your encouragement.]

During his last few days in Tijuana, Dan grew even weaker. He knew that things in his body were not going in the right direction. He had no appetite. He had some internal bleeding. As the doctors explained, "Your disease is not responding to the treatment this time in the way we would have desired." Even in the midst of his physical situation, Dan's heart continued to focus on God, which his last entry from Mexico reflects:

February 9th, 2003

Today, I choose to be thankful. For sun and a bright blue sky. For the knowledge that the God who created the sun and sky has made me the object of His affection. For the passionate, relentless love of Jesus. For a Savior who suffered and died for my sin so I wouldn't have to. For the presence of God in my hospital room.

For a deep breath without pain. For the privilege of sleeping without coughing last night, in response to the prayers of God's people. For a hospital where the president prays daily for each patient. For the knowledge that my life is in the hands of the Great Physician. For the peace of surrender and the joy of resting in the arms of my Savior. For the promise of eternity in His presence, where there is fullness of joy and pleasures forever. For the assurance that I will not be tied to this weak and failing body forever—but that one day I'll be recreated. When that happens, I'll be a white man who can jump.

For my boys who tell me they love me to infinity and beyond every day. Some days it's Cozumel and beyond, too, depending on whichever seems further. For my wife—my

*helpmate, my best friend, my nurse, and more
often than not, a rock to lean on. When I am
in pain, to look into her eyes is like looking at
Jesus. For the friends who have come across the
country to stay by me in my room—Paul, Bar-
ry, George, Ross, Dave, and the many others
who have offered to come. For the unbelievable
bond I share with each brother and sister who
names the name of Jesus. For my parents and
in-laws and brothers and sisters and all sorts of
family who keep loving and praying and calling and hoping.*

*For a God who provides and for people who
graciously and unselfishly offer what they have
to be used by Him for His purposes. For 400
high school students who gave $10,000. For
people I have never met who have sent cards
and letters, which now fill an entire wall of my
hospital room. For poems from tenderhearted
kids. For thousands of people who bless me
by praying for me and my family and writing
notes of encouragement on the web page. For a
God who would use the technology of the Internet to create a community of prayers.*

*For the privilege of being part of the grand
and glorious plan of the Almighty God, a plan*

that was established before the earth's founda-
tions, one where every day of my life was writ-
ten in His book before one of them ever came to
be. For the joy of knowing that today matters,
my life matters, my thoughts matter, and that
even today, God's plan to use me for His glory
is unfolding in my life.

If you think to pray for me today, just thank
God for blessing me.

FARGO OR BUST

After he returned home, Dan's condition continued
to decline. He was in and out of the hospital several
times during the next month. Even in the midst of
raging fevers and a hacking cough, God continued
to open doors for Dan to be used mightily for His
glory—and Dan never backed away. He forged
ahead in faithful devotion and service to Christ.
One powerful example was Dan's ministry at an
Integrity Music worship event in Fargo, ND, about
a three-hour drive from Dan's home.

February 25th, 2003

Here's a God thing: This Sunday night, my
friend Dave Lubben is recording a live worship
album for Integrity in Fargo, ND. He asked a

few weeks ago if I would share a brief message with the audience. I smiled and thought, Yeah, right. *I told him sincerely that if God gave me the strength to do it, I'd be there. I never anticipated this would happen.*

A few days ago, I shared the invitation with another friend. I told him I thought I might be able to get up there if I were able to lie down the whole ride there and back. He said, "How about a motorhome?"

I said, "That would be great." I did not expect to be able to find a motorhome that would suddenly be made available to us. The very next day my friend (Paul) was talking to a friend of his who said he happened to be buying a motorhome that night, and that if we wanted to use it, it was ours for free.

I don't know if God wants me there or not. Right now I feel like brushing my teeth is a monumental challenge. I share this with you so that you can pray and ask the Lord to make His perfect will clear. Interestingly, Integrity is considering naming this recording project "A Place Called Surrender," the same title as my book. In a few months, this CD will be all over the world, spreading the glory of God. I love

seeing Him work and sliding into His plan,
wherever that is, even if only for five minutes
at a time!

March 5th, 2003

Thank you for all who prayed for Sunday
night. Many miracles happened! We set out in
the motorhome from the Twin Cities with a
convoy of about 25 people, and had other fam-
ily members who joined us in Fargo.

We arrived safely and they wheeled me into
the auditorium just as the event was starting.
It was very emotional for me to see how pow-
erfully God was using Dave and his music. My
thoughts went back to the week that we met at
a camp in the middle of North Dakota. Nei-
ther of us had any confidence in our ability to
minister, and God used our weakness to show
Himself strong that week. Revival broke out
among those students. The amazing thing was,
even though he was a gifted vocalist and gui-
tar player, Dave had never before led worship.
He didn't know any songs. He brought a large
folder of transparencies and asked me which
ones we should do—about an hour before the
first session! That was the first time Dave said

"yes" to God about leading worship, and now God was using his willing heart to reach the masses through this recording.

Dave introduced me halfway through the program and invited me to come and share with the audience. I picked up my Bible, and Tammy helped me up onto the stage. I had no message to share, because I had wanted to prepare on Friday and Saturday. The only problem was that I hadn't gotten out of bed at all on Saturday, and only for a moment on Friday. I had just been way too sick. I had absolutely nothing planned. But when I settled into my chair on stage with my Bible in hand, God gave me a message that came without thinking. I felt supernatural strength to get up and walk as well as to share. Before I was introduced, I had no energy at all—I just wanted to lie down.

It was a wonderful blessing to be a part of the whole event. I know God wanted us there. I have no other way to explain how or why He would provide all the resources to make it happen, and the strength to do it, or the words to communicate what was on His heart. God wanted us there, and He wanted to bless us by allowing us to be there. And bless us He did!

A WIDER AUDIENCE

After the trip to Fargo, Dan was drained. He was staying in bed and eating very little. It was hard to imagine that he had just testified in front of 800 people when he could barely walk across the room. And during this time of weakness, an unexpected call came. A reporter from the Minneapolis *Star Tribune* wanted to do a feature article on Dan. She had already read his website journal and interviewed several of his friends. Now she wanted to talk to Dan. When the scheduled time for the interview came, Dan was back in the hospital and at times unresponsive. His kidneys were failing. The reporter visited Dan at his bedside, and God opened a brief window of clarity and focus for Dan. He responded to her questions and once again testified of God's faithful love in his life.

Several days later, the article appeared in the newspaper, and within less than a week there were more than 10,000 hits on Dan's website. Old friends, total strangers, people from other states, people from other countries—all were signing the website guestbook to leave messages of encouragement and testimonies of how God had used the article and the website in their lives. One college friend who had lost touch with Dan and was now a missionary in Kenya had just acquired Internet access. He saw Dan's story when he logged on to read the Minneapolis paper. A Hindu lady in India came across the website by "accident" while looking for news about world events. Once again, the books sold out as people wanted to learn more about Dan and the amazing God who had sustained him through this adversity. In Dan's weakest hour, God's power through him was exploding.

CHAPTER 17

STILL HIS

Dan had persistently shared his journey with any-one who wanted to hear. He had opened his heart and his life through posting regular updates on the website, and so many people had responded to his transparency and his faith.

Understandably, the number of his postings decreased as his condition worsened, but anytime he had a lucid moment, he was eager to open his laptop and type out his heart. Even in his final en-tries, his message was noticeably consistent. After sixteen months of battling cancer, his desire had not changed.

February 27th, 2003

The last fever of the day is on its way out,

and I'm having a rare moment where the pain is minimal. I am awake, I'm not coughing, and I am thinking fairly clearly. (I guess that's debatable—my point being that many times in the last few weeks I haven't been able to put two sentences together in my head.)

It's in a window of opportunity like this that I want to pull out my Bible and make up for lost time in seeking the Lord. I am reminded that our relationship with Him is so much more about what He is doing in pursuing us and shaping us and teaching us and loving us than it is about what we are doing. If the basis for my relationship with Him were about what I am doing, I would not have a relationship with Him right now. I feel like I have not offered Him one thing in the last month. For the most part, my focus has been on lumps, pain, blood, scans, and drugs.

The beauty of grace is that God loves me on the days when I worship Him with great perspective, and He loves me on the days when I care about nothing other than getting rid of pain. I could not choose between these days as to which would find Him loving me more.

There are days when God reveals truth to me

from Scripture and I get excited about it and I find great joy in sharing that with as many as I can. These are wonderful days—days when the suffering seems to have meaning and make sense, at least for a moment. There are other days when I can't make sense of any of it, and all I see is pain. My own physical pain. The pain in my wife's eyes as she struggles daily to yield her husband to God. The pain I see all around me in the others suffering at the hospital. I do not feel like a godly, spiritual man on these days.

However, the truth about me and the truth about God is that my hope is not in me or my ability to follow God or love Him or worship Him. My hope is in God's ability to love me, to draw me to Himself, to accomplish His purposes in my life. I have been encouraged by Psalm 91 on so many occasions since being diagnosed, and verse 4 has become especially meaningful. "He will cover you with His feathers, and under His wings you will find refuge; His faithfulness will be your shield and rampart." Not my faithfulness to Him. HIS faithfulness to me! This is our hope in Christ! The pressure is no longer on us. It is not up to us, because we have put our hope in one greater than us.

I cannot save my life by eating the right foods or taking the right supplements. For Pete's sake, I can't even eat right now. The pressure is not on me to find the right doctor. I don't have to follow a formula that will assure me of God's healing blessing to be released. My hope is in His faithfulness.

Maybe I'm just beginning to understand a little bit about grace, because I feel totally empty-handed before God tonight—like I have absolutely nothing to offer Him but selfishness and pride and a bunch of crud—and yet I know that He totally delights in me in spite of all this. He is and will be faithful to me. I am still the object of His affection. I am still the apple of His eye. I am still His.

I have very few assurances for tomorrow, but I do know that I will still belong to Jesus. Regardless of my attitude toward Him or anyone else tomorrow, He will still be passionately pursuing me. He will still be in love with me. In the midst of whatever my body is going through, this assurance will be enough.

I guess that is my prayer request: that I would celebrate the love and faithfulness of God regardless of what happens in my body.

And God answered Dan's prayer. During his final days, Dan never lashed out in anger. He never lost his grateful spirit. He rejoiced in the Lord's love to the very end. When he could no longer pray, he would nod in agreement as others offered adoration to God. When he could no longer sing, he would lift his weak hands in worship to the Lord as praise CDs played in his hospital room. And on his 33rd birthday, Dan left what he used to call the "shadows" to finally experience the real thing. His friend Ross posted the following web entry that day:

March 20th, 2003

Dan is with Jesus. Around 10:30 this morning, Dan finally saw with his own eyes everything he has believed in and lived for. He did not struggle. He died very peacefully. He wasn't fighting. He was free.

I am so happy for Dan.

Hundreds and hundreds of people filed through the church on Sunday afternoon for Dan's visitation. One after another, they testified of how God had used Dan to draw them into a closer relationship with the Lord. Two former youth group students told how they are now youth pastors and are modeling their ministry after Dan's. Close to a thousand people gathered the following day for Dan's memorial and celebration service. Tears of joy and tears of loss flowed together as friends and family reflected on Dan's life and worshiped his great God. The message of surrender to God was proclaimed, the invitation presented, and once again, people responded with personal faith and abandon to Jesus Christ.

A CALL TO SURRENDER

I am no resident of this place called Surrender. Actually, I wouldn't even visit unless God took me there. But each time I begin to taste of it, to taste of Him, it creates a hunger for more. More and more, the words of David have become the expression of my heart when he says, "Your love is better than life." (Psalm 63:3)

Do you hear God speaking to you? Do you see Him pursuing you in the events of your life? While your story may be different than mine, I have no doubt that His goal is the same. Accept His invitation to draw near to Him . . . to come to a place . . . called Surrender.

Dan Roelofs

CHAPTER 18

HOPE FOR LIFE

[This chapter was written by Ross Robinson, Dan's dear friend, shortly after Dan went to be with the Lord.]

As a pastor, I deal with pain and suffering and death regularly and up close, and it hurts. It really hurts. My heart has often ached with others in their times of loss. But I have to tell you, when you lose your own soul friend to cancer, it feels like the hardest thing in the world. The pain hits you like a truck and keeps pounding you like a hammer. It's not logical and it's not controllable. It feels awful and unbearable. On the outside, life rushes on at 90 mph, but on the inside things feel like they are in slow motion, sometimes standing still. Everything seems changed. Pain is at every turn. And there's nothing to do except cling to God.

As I faced the reality that Dan had a serious and aggressive cancer, I anticipated times of confusion and fear in my own heart—and I knew I needed God's perspective. I knew I needed truth to protect me from being swept away by doubt and deceit, so I opened my Bible and dove in.

I had read 1 Corinthians 15 many times. I had even used it to comfort others in seasons of loss. Now I was holding to it as tightly as I could. In fact, I turned to that passage and said, "God, I need to understand how You view Dan's situation, and I am camping out in this chapter until You penetrate my heart and mind with its truth. You have to help me see this situation from Your vantage point."

He has been doing just that. He is helping me realize the very real hope I have because of Christ's resurrection. When Jesus walked out of the grave, He did so in victory over death. None of us who believe in Jesus can be defeated by death. It's impossible. As final as death seems and as awful as it feels to lose someone we love, death ultimately cannot win. Jesus has already won that battle for all who trust in Him.

The New Testament believers referred to death

as sleep. That's really how they viewed it—like a nap. It is a time when our spirits are immediately with the Lord (which has to be awesome), but also a time when our bodies are waiting to be resurrected—perfect and imperishable—to be reunited with our spirits and live forever with the Lord (which has to be even more awesome!). God has promised that death is not the end.

If we really believe that about the future, it will affect the way we live today. A confidence in God's promise provides us with a comfort and a security that free us to risk everything now for the sake of Christ. No matter what happens, we can't lose and our behavior will testify to that.

Paul said it this way in 1 Corinthians 15, "I die daily." In other words, "I surrender." He not only understood the truth of his own future victory over death, but he embraced that reality as his motto for life. As a result, Paul did crazy things for the sake of God's kingdom! He valued what God had promised in the future more than his current comfort or happiness. He chose to lay it all down every day. "I die daily." For Paul, that meant beatings and imprisonments and shipwrecks, so that others could experience the grace and forgiveness of God. For Dan it meant cancer.

That's surrender—the freedom to give it all to God because whatever road it takes us down, surrender can only lead to joy and life forever. That's where God is calling us. Not to mere resignation. That would be a discouraging way to exist. It's so much more. It's a place of anticipation and hope. It's a place of true freedom.

For most of us, our paths won't be the same as the Apostle Paul's or Dan's. God is not calling us to that same sacrifice. He's calling us to another place—another place with the same name.

A place called Surrender.

Ross Robinson, May 2003

This is my earnest expectation and my hope, that with all boldness, Christ will even now be exalted in my body, whether by life or by death. For to me to live is Christ and to die is gain. (Philippians 1:20-21)

Dan and his faithful friend, Ross Robinson [2001]

CHAPTER 19

MY TRIBUTE

[This chapter was written by Tammy shortly
after Dan went to be with the Lord.]

What a tremendous honor and privilege it has been
for me to journey with Dan as his wife. I consider
myself blessed beyond measure for the years God
gave us together. Dan had a contagiousness about
him. He loved life, and could make me laugh like
no one I'd ever met. He could take an unpleasant
situation and find something fun in it. His spirit
was filled with grace and patience, always able to
find the best in people. I have never met anyone
who did not like Dan. After spending time with
him, you would walk away somehow feeling valued
and important. Dan just brought out the best in

people. He had a comfortable confidence properly placed in his identity as a child of God. This led him to be truly authentic and transparent with people he knew and met.

The way Dan lived his life in front of others was the same way he lived in our home as husband and father, behind closed doors. Dan was very devoted to our family. Dan desired the best for us, so he passionately prayed for our hearts to be growing in the Lord. He was my soul mate, companion, and faithful friend. He sacrificially made time to be with his boys, Taylor and Reid. He loved reading to them, playing ball with them, taking them for bike rides, going to the park, and camping out in our backyard. Most of all, Dan loved teaching his boys about Jesus. It was no secret how much he loved them. His conversations were filled with stories of his boys and what he was learning from God through them. Taylor and Reid were his pride and joy! They truly are blessed to have had a daddy who loved them so much.

Dan's time on Earth was short, but the legacy he left is so rich and it continues on in our hearts. This legacy is extremely powerful because of the God Dan found, a God he could trust with his life.

God's Word was Dan's lifeline and was what gave him the confidence to trust in His sovereign plan. During his last days on this earth, Dan never reacted with anger or frustration, even though he desperately wanted to live. He wrote in his journal,

I have no question about God's love or His presence. I guess this is what it means to walk by faith and not by sight—you bank on what you know is true, even though your feelings are telling you to abandon ship.

Being assured of God's best for him, Dan was able to come to a place where he found peace in surrendering his life to his Savior.

I am forever changed because of this journey on which God has taken us. Dan helped me to truly see Jesus. Because of his life, I am realizing the importance of treasuring God's truth in my heart and mind. I am also learning how important it is for me to take time to be still in God's presence, to hear His voice and allow His Word to speak to me. By faith, I am trusting that God has a plan and purpose for my life. As difficult as it is to understand the whys, I am putting my trust in His faithfulness to me and my boys. What God has for us is better than anything we could want for ourselves. I know that God is with me and He is good.

Dan, I will forever love you! Thank you for showing me what it is to live life wholeheartedly for Jesus.

I pray that, until we meet again, I will faithfully remain in this place called Surrender!

Tammy Roelofs, May 2003

"Because of the Lord's great love we are not consumed, for His compassions never fail. They are new every morning; great is Your faithfulness." (Lamentations 3:22-23)

Dan loved the game! [1988]

The Roelofs Family – Jim, Jan, Dan, Mark, Rachel
[1992]

Falling in Love [1992]

Our Wedding Day [August 7, 1993]

Making memories together at Lake George [1999]

[2000]

Dan cherished his boys [1999]

[2001]

168

Christmas Day [2001]

Trusting God [2004]

Scotty enters our lives

[2005]

And the story continues . . . [2015]

Sibling love - Taylor, Reid, and Rylee [2015]

Taylor with the interception [2015]

Touchdown Reid [2015]

THE STORY BEHIND DAN'S STORY
By Tammy Roelofs Kessler

June 2016

When Dan was alive, he was always the writer and speaker. I was more than happy to let him have the stage, with me supporting him in the comfort of the background. However, in the years since Dan's passing—and as this book has been passed on to more and more people—it seems that God has had other ideas. God's plans have a way of doing that, don't they? They tend to push us outside of our comfort zones, like me stepping forward to write these last few pages of Dan's re-released book.

A great number of people who have read this book have shared many amazing, encouraging stories with me. I am so incredibly grateful for each story, for each person who took the time to write or walk up and share his or her heart. I have been humbled and honored to hear how these precious people have valued Dan's words and life as we did, and still do.

Over the years, I've often been asked questions from people sincerely wanting to know how we are doing. Because I've heard so many, I feel I need to answer some of the most asked questions that may come up for you as well after reading this book. In doing so, you'll learn some of the "stories behind the story." And, I will also answer perhaps the most personal of questions that I'm often asked, "So, how are you and your family doing today?"

I'll end with that question. But for now, let me start by sharing with you some of the backstory to what led us to surrender, and how that changed our lives so deeply.

How did you experience God's comfort and strength as Dan grew weaker?

While hospitals have never been my favorite place, I remember one day feeling strongly that we were on holy ground. I felt like angels were ministering to Dan – and I could feel God's presence. In fact, I remember the Lord's gentle whisper coming through my mind so clearly one night, saying, *This is not in*

174

vain. Those words pierced my heart.

In the months that followed, that phrase became one of the main comforts the Lord whispered over and over to me. It is a truth He is still confirming for me today. I'm so thankful for what God gave me in that moment in the hospital. Live or die, none of this would be in vain. He had a plan.

Did Dan help you prepare for life without him?
As Dan's cancer progressed, we held to the hope that he would be healed, and that someday he would walk right out of the hospital. We believed for a miracle, knowing God was able to do immeasurably more than we could ask or imagine.

There was one day Dan was very open about "what next," should the Lord take him home. He was convinced that I would marry again and I was convinced I couldn't envision being married to anyone else but him. While he was aware that he might not grow old with me, or be able to raise his boys as they grew up, he truly wanted us to be loved, cherished, and taken care of. That was his heart.

Once, when Dan was still well enough to be at home, we had a conversation where Dan urged me to go to the Lord instead of him. It wasn't that he didn't want to be there for me, but I sensed he was preparing me to depend on God instead of him. I remember thinking, *No, I want YOU and YOUR perspective!* Sensing my struggle, Dan spoke the following words, and then lovingly wrote them down on a notecard for me:

Where we choose to focus will determine our feelings. If we focus on what we fear and worry about the worst possible outcome, we will be consumed with negative emotions. However, we can choose to focus on God—His unfailing love, His goodness, His unwavering commitment to us, His infinite strength, and His promise to provide for us. We need to choose to praise Him, regardless of how we feel. His victory over fear and death and Satan is our victory.

The truth in Dan's words gave me hope. I immediately hung up the notecard, and still have it today.

Dan was human wasn't he? Didn't he have bad days? Didn't he want to give up?
Dan was human, and there were many tough days. But Dan always had fight in him. There was one time during an especially rough round of treatment that Dan wanted to give up, but God gave him the

grace to get through it.

The Dan you read about was exactly the same man behind closed doors as he was in public. He never walked a double life. He just was who he was. Reading the Bible and journaling was a daily part of his life. As you've read, writing was one of the main ways he connected with God and processed what he was going through.

Dan's writing ends before his final days. Can you share with us about your experiences at that time?
"God, give me the grace for whatever happens today." That was my prayer as I entered the hospital on March 20, 2003.

When I arrived in Dan's room, I was greeted by my parents and Dan's parents, who let me know that Dan had died just minutes before I arrived. In that moment, I knew what I had to do—pray to see if God would choose to bring him back to us. I told everyone in the room that I needed some time alone with Dan. As they left, I walked over to him and was overcome with emotion as I realized, *He's gone . . . it really happened?* I prayed, "God, I have 20 minutes of faith to see if You will choose to send him back."

You see, throughout Dan's entire battle with cancer, I always believed deep down that he would be healed. In the face of every discouraging doctor's report, I continued to believe that God could heal him for His glory. God wouldn't really allow him to die, would He? Wouldn't it be more impactful for him to be healed? Why would God choose to take someone so passionate for Christ, with so much influence?

Standing there in Dan's hospital room, in the midst of death, I believed that God might choose to give Dan a supernatural heaven experience and then send him back to us. We've all heard stories of people on their deathbed going to see Jesus, and coming back to testify. I believed Dan could be one of those people. So, I prayed, and I hoped for a miracle. I held Dan's hand and waited in anticipation for a sign of life, for his eyes to open and his once strong hand to squeeze mine in return. After praying, I leaned over him and opened one of his eyelids.

Dan had always had the most beautiful, crystal blue eyes I'd ever seen. When cancer overtook his body, his eyes had become a cloudy blue, a result of the cancer. But on this day, after his heart stopped beating, his eyes were brilliant blue once again. Their clarity had returned. In my spirit, it was confirmation that he was with Jesus. I felt like God had spoken. This was His will for us. Dan was gone.

I sat down in a chair in his hospital room and did the only thing I knew to do: surrender to God's plan for my life. I lifted my hands and held my palms upward. "I receive this, God. I have to believe this is from You."

What was it like going home after the funeral?
The day after the funeral, everyone went home. My family lived two hours away, and Dan's lived five hours away. They were tired. I was tired. It was the first time in months that I was truly alone.

The morning after the funeral, I organized my kitchen cabinets. Initially, I found that getting busy with anything was therapeutic. Focusing on anything other than myself seemed to keep me from being consumed by sadness. I also focused much of my attention on the boys. Even though I was no longer a wife, I was still a mother, and that gave me something to focus on each day. During this time, our church family rallied around us. These dear friends filled many of the gaps left by Dan's passing, and their support had a profound impact on my family.

One of the hardest parts of grieving a loved one

is the loss of shared moments no one else knows. Those were the times I felt the most alone. For me, time stood still when I was grieving. It was like being in a time warp, simply surviving each day. Some days, the most I could do was feel thankful for each breath. I'd offer my next breath to the Lord, because at times that was all I could give. And, by God's grace, that was enough. The days, weeks, and months passed, and eventually we found our new "normal."

What was the healing process like?
By His great mercy, in the initial months after Dan died, God enabled me to put my grief on hold to focus on my boys and their needs. I poured all my energy into them. Once I felt reassured that they were doing better, God allowed my pain to come to the surface so He could begin the process of healing me.

But initially it didn't feel like healing. Feeling the weight of my own grief was overwhelming. And for the first time in my life, I had (what I assumed was) a full on panic attack. I didn't know what to do. Crazy as it sounds, the first thought that came to my mind was to go to the computer and type out all of my feelings.

I bawled my eyes out to the Lord. After the purging of every emotion I could think of, I was physically weak from crying. But, miraculously, the anxiety was gone; my heartbeat returned to normal.

A few weeks later, I had another panic attack. I went back to my computer again, and this time I decided to write to Dan. Everything came out— from sadness, to frustration, to telling him I did not want to raise the kids alone. It was incredibly hard, but incredibly healing.

I don't remember being mad at God. For me, the act of surrendering was easier than the option of being mad. There is peace in surrender. If I'm mad at God, I'm just stuck, and hurting—and hurt people hurt people. I didn't want that for myself or my boys. That didn't mean it was all easy. There were times I would lay on the floor or in my bed and cry—hard. But, I learned when the pain or anxiety came to let it out.

I vividly remember one incredible moment in the months following Dan's death, sitting on my bed having some quiet time with the Lord and thanking Him for the closeness I felt with Him. I knew I wouldn't have known Him the way I did in that moment if Dan hadn't passed. "Thank you for letting me experience this," I prayed sincerely. Never did I think I would ever thank God for taking my husband, but I was thankful for the intimacy He had revealed to me in my heartache. It took the loss of my husband for me to experience the full richness and authenticity of God's overwhelming love and peace. *I don't ever want to lose this*, I thought. *I don't ever want to be too comfortable again.*

In the difficult times following Dan's death, what gave you the most hope and encouragement?
After Dan passed away, there were times I felt like the weight of sadness and grief threatened to overtake me. For some reason, talking with people didn't really help. The overwhelming grief actually caused the muscles in my chest—around my heart—to ache for over a year.

Worship was the only thing that lifted the heaviness from my heart. I would raise my hands and sing at the top of my lungs. During the most difficult days, that was the ONLY thing that helped. Worship music soothed my spirit and helped me cope. It brought me into such a place of calm—even moments of joy! It was an indescribable feeling, and one that can only be explained as God's peace that passes understanding. I would turn on the music and it would drown out the sorrow. It would release the physical pressure I carried in my chest, and I would weep as I cried out to God. Those moments felt like miracles—that during the saddest, darkest time of my life, worshipping my Savior could pull me out of my sorrow and make me feel like we were going to make it!

When I look back at all of it, I recognized it was a battle for the mind, a battle to believe God's truth and not the debilitating lies of fear and despair. I had been a pastor's wife for years, but it wasn't until those desperate moments of praise and worship that I realized the power of truth to fully defeat fear. I saw first hand that the power of God works! I needed to make a choice. I could choose to let despair and fear take over. Or I could choose to stop and focus on the TRUTH of what God said.

How are you and your boys doing now? Really?
While there is so much I could share about how good God has been to us since this journey with cancer, I want to re-emphasize the phrase that has sustained me through it all: this was not in vain! And I'm blessed—abundantly blessed. Thank you, God.

There were times when I honestly didn't know why we were doing as well as we were. Don't get me wrong. I cried. I mourned. I had moments of frustration and questioning. But there was something so special and supernatural about it all, this undeniable covering. I knew it was God's plan, even though I didn't like it. I knew we were going to be okay. We even found moments of thankfulness in the most difficult times. To me, that's grace.

God brought a wonderful man into my life who loves me, and loves the boys as if they were his own. God expanded my heart to love another man, and Scott Kessler and I were married in 2006. Seven years later, we were blessed with a beautiful daughter, Rylee Grace, who completed our family and fills our home with so much joy.

Taylor and Reid are both men now, following Jesus and thriving in their own unique ways. Taylor is attending Whitworth University, studying Kinesiology and playing college football. Reid is at Southern Nazarene University, pursuing a degree in Communications and also playing college football.

As our story of surrender continues to be written, I am certain that all of God's promises remain true—even though my life looks very different than what I expected. God has not answered all of my prayers the way I wanted, but He has never abandoned me. He is always faithful, and His promises are true. Despite heartache, loss, and grief, I believe God is still in control, and He is good. This is my own personal place called Surrender.

He has always had a beautiful plan. Creating beauty from ashes. Restoring all things for His glory. This was not just for Dan's legacy, but for my future, and our boys' as well. That is grace. And hope. And so much love.

"For I know the plans I have for you," declares the Lord, "Plans to prosper you and not to harm you, plans to give you a hope and a future."
(Jeremiah 29:11)

"So do not fear, for I am with you;
do not be dismayed,
for I am your God.
I will strengthen you and help you;
I will uphold you with my righteous right hand."
(Isaiah 41:10)

186

CPSIA information can be obtained
at www.ICGtesting.com
Printed in the USA
LVHW081744290521
688881LV00015B/1149